WOVEN FOR HIS PURPOSE

Embracing the Gift of
Unconditional Love God has for You

ERNA BOEHS

Published by hope*books
2217 Matthews Township Pkwy
Suite D302
Matthews, NC 28105
www.hopebooks.com

hope*books is a division of hope*media

Printed in the United States of America

First paperback edition.
Paperback ISBN: 979-8-89185-218-1
Hardcover ISBN: 979-8-89185-187-0
Ebook ISBN: 979-8-89185-188-7
Library of Congress Number: 2025936293

Endorsements

Woven for His Purpose is a powerful and inspiring book that guides readers on a journey of faith, self-discovery, and transformation. Erna's vulnerability and wisdom shine through as she shares how she overcame self-doubt and limiting beliefs to embrace the life God called her to live. As someone who has had the privilege of mentoring Erna, I have witnessed her incredible growth firsthand. This book is a testament to her faith, resilience, and commitment to empowering others. Readers will find practical insights, heartfelt encouragement, and a profound reminder that they are never alone on their journey.

—**Dani Medrano**
The Metaphysical Performance Coach

Woven for His Purpose is a must-read for anyone desiring to move their life forward with wisdom and intentional joy. Lessons and guidance shared from someone's lived experience holds the power to transform lives…having watched Erna develop this book, I can attest that what you have in your hands is just that! *Woven for His Purpose* is a unique guide (truly lived by an author who is as hope-filled as she is upbeat) written to help you pursue God's grace as you grow in your own special purpose.

—**Holly Pickerel**
ICF Certified Life Coach & Personal Development Mentor

In *Woven for His Purpose*, Erna Boehs beautifully shares her life experiences—her joys, struggles, and faith—revealing how God weaves purpose through even the most difficult seasons. As she writes, "God has a way of weaving purpose through even the craziest and most difficult parts of our life." Her transparent storytelling invites readers to journey alongside her, reflecting on their own lives as she weaves together the threads of faith, growth, and grace. With thoughtful questions at the end of each chapter, this book is not just an inspiring read but also a powerful tool for personal reflection or small group study. Thank you, Erna, for enriching many lives with your words of truth and encouragement.

—Terry Deason
Illuminate the Path Coaching

Having walked through a personal growth journey right alongside Erna through years of a special friendship and business partnership, I've watched her focus on stepping into what God has called her to be. I've watched her refreshing relationship with God guide her as He pulls her closer. Erna has an infectious personality that comes through as her stories come to life. You will smile reading them. This book is a soul-searching guide that will also pull you to God and inspire you to want to join her on the incredible journey of authenticity.

—Nicole Lamar
Artist, Creator of MORE

Woven for His Purpose is a masterpiece—like a quilt made from the scrap pieces of everyday life. Erna's vulnerability and faith-filled storytelling beautifully reflect how God makes beauty from ashes. I saw myself in so many of her words, especially in the chapter on grace, which deeply touched my heart. Her thoughtful questions will help me grow and reflect, and her journey reminded me that through faith, we find strength, healing, and hope.

—Michelle Stanford Camp

This book is a powerful reminder of the beauty and strength found in vulnerability. Erna's honest stories and faith-filled reflections encouraged me deeply. The writing is heartfelt and easy to connect with, and the Bible verses are so thoughtfully placed. I especially appreciated the reflection questions and look forward to revisiting them with loved ones. Her testimony of God's love and faithfulness is both inspiring and comforting.

—Brittany Schrock

This book is a powerful testimony of strength and healing. The author's willingness to share her story with such vulnerability is truly inspiring. Each section is thoughtfully laid out, making it easy for readers to reflect and grow through their own journey. I'm deeply grateful for the courage it took to write these words—this book is a gift to anyone seeking hope and restoration. .

—Wanda Kyle

Dedication

To my husband and children—my greatest blessings and my daily reminders of God's love. Your unwavering love, support, and faith have made this journey a joy. May you always know how deeply you are loved.

To every woman who has ever felt unseen, weary, or burdened by expectations—you are not alone. You are so cherished, loved with an all-encompassing love, and created for a purpose far greater than you can imagine. May this book remind you to release the weight of *doing it all* and embrace His unconditional love, rest, and the freedom found in Him.

To my dad, who had a love for writing but never saw his words shared with the world—this book is in honor of you. Your passion for writing left an imprint on my life, and in some way, I hope this carries forward the love of words that was in you.

To my mom, who raised us to be faithful in what we believe, to work hard, and to be diligent in all we do—thank you for your example of strength and devotion.

Acknowledgments

Writing this book has been a journey of learning, growing, believing, and trusting, and I could not have done it alone.

To my husband, Terry—thank you for supporting me every step of the way with your unwavering belief, love, and even traveling with me as I worked on crafting this book. Your encouragement has meant more than words can express.

To my wonderful children, Nicolee, Carlee, Connor, and Natalie—thank you for believing in my dream and supporting me throughout this journey. You helped keep the home fires burning while I spent time writing and traveling, and I am so grateful for your love and patience.

To my family and friends—those who checked in, asked about my writing, and encouraged me along the way—you know who you are, and I am incredibly grateful for your belief in this story. Each word of encouragement and every question about my progress reminded me that this book mattered.

A special thank you to Kathrine Lee and the Pure Hope Ranch, where I attended my first writing workshop—the place where I took my first steps on the author's path.

To hope*books, my publishing company—thank you for providing a space to bring this book to life and for believing in our hope stories. A heartfelt thanks to my editors for your thoughtful insights and expertise in refining my words. And to Hope Dover, who kept track of the many moving pieces in this process—your dedication and organization are so appreciated.

To my incredible life coaches and mentors—you have poured wisdom, encouragement, and belief into me and my book. Your guidance has shaped not only my writing but also the person I am becoming. I may not be able to name each of you individually, but please know that your impact is deeply felt and profoundly appreciated.

To the many authors whose words have encouraged me on this journey—your stories and insights reminded me that writing is not only possible but meaningful. A special thank you to Emily P. Freeman, whose work first exposed me to the idea that I could write. Starting with blogging, I found my voice, which ultimately led to the dream of writing this book.

To my readers—this book is for you. Your hunger for truth, growth, and the freedom found in Christ has compelled me to write these words. I pray this book continues to bless you, remind you that you are deeply loved, and assure you that you are never alone on this journey.

I am also deeply thankful for my dad. Though he is no longer with us, he had a love for writing and always wanted to write a book of his own. I wish his story could have been written, and in a small way, I hope this book carries a piece of him forward.

Above all, I give thanks to God—the One who has been weaving my life from the very beginning with unconditional love and purpose. He reminds me daily that we are meant for more and that the path we walk is one best traveled with Him as our ultimate source and guide.

Table of Contents

The Beginning

---

*"For you created my inmost being; you knit me together in
my mother's womb. I praise you because I am fearfully and
wonderfully made; your works are wonderful, I know that
full well."*
—Psalm 139:13–14

My life began in the backcountry of a little village in Paraguay,
South America. Dad, an American boy, had moved there with his
parents, while Mom came to work for his mom as a young helper.
Eventually, they got married, and so began our family. When I was
almost five years old, we moved to the United States, a transition
that brought challenges for all of us. Mom had to learn the language alongside us children. Spanish was our native language, but
through the years, we lost much of it, much to Dad's dismay. I've
been working to relearn it. The language feels like a thread from
my past, woven deep but frayed from lack of use. I can often understand it, though at times, if the pace feels too fast, it's like trying to
untangle a knot in a tapestry.

Adjusting to life in the States brought a few difficult years as a
child. Starting school while still learning English was a challenge. I
often mixed English and Spanish, particularly in how I structured
sentences, which then came out backwards. My memories of childhood are not as clear as I would like them to be. As I write, though,
there are vague memories that become clearer. Reflecting brings

clarity, allowing the design of what God has been weaving to become more vibrant. I remember that I didn't like some of my older cousins at first. Dad would take me to their house to walk to school with them. To me, they were strangers, big and intimidating. Dad knew them well, and they were family to him, but my young mind saw them as scary, hairy boys. Isn't it interesting how our perceptions can shape the images we see? Over time, these threads of fear and unfamiliarity were woven into trust and comfort, and I came to realize they were kind and good people—people who would do anything to help out.

My first three years of schooling were in a one-room schoolhouse, the same one my dad had attended as a boy. I liked my teacher; she was strict but fair, managing a classroom with multiple grades. I was a good student and made decent grades. If I had continued in that school, I believe I would have maintained my academic success.

However, the next three years brought new challenges: three different teachers and a different environment that wasn't always conducive to learning. There was unrest in the three families and our homes. We were trying to live in a perfect world that didn't exist, a world where everyone did what they were supposed to do and everyone was happy.

These years felt like a tangled mess of threads, where harmony was elusive and the design for our lives seemed unclear. I can only imagine what that must have been like for my parents with seven children and more coming in the future. I was the oldest of ten children, my parents endeavoring to raise a family without clear directions on where or how to live. It had to have been so difficult, but I know God had a path for all of us. It may have taken some of us a good, long time to finally catch on, but He is good and patient with us.

This group, The Church of God in Christ Mennonite (also known as Holdeman Mennonites), had previous connections with Dad. At one point, he had even considered joining them. However, family members and others who had once been part of the group discouraged him from doing so. They saw the Holdeman Mennonites as too liberal, accusing them of manipulating people into membership and having underlying issues that weren't immediately visible.

I realize now that every church group has things that may not make sense at first. Every denomination, every faith tradition, is shaped by human understanding and sometimes by human limitations. But I truly believe that most people are doing the best they can with what they know and how they interpret Scripture. This is my personal belief; I know some would disagree.

It's easy to criticize a group we don't understand or disagree with, but at the end of the day, what does that really accomplish? God is the ultimate truth, and His way is the true foundation. Churches are made up of imperfect people, each with their own convictions, struggles, and blind spcts. And none of us—no group, no denomination—can take credit for redemption. That belongs to God alone.

Eventually, Dad's brother and cousin left for the Holdeman Mennonite community. They likely had many of the same questions and reservations that Dad would have had. There were certain practices within the group that he had strong feelings about—things like men's haircuts, the way they trimmed their beards (Dad didn't believe in ever cutting your beard), and the way the women dressed. Once again, I have to point out that Dad was doing the best he knew, just like we all are.

In the end, Dad never joined them. Instead, he worked alongside several men who were Holdeman Mennonites until he started his own business—a business where we, as his children, often helped. He was a carpenter, but primarily replaced old roofing. Dad was a hardworking man who believed in doing things well. His diligence and work ethic became threads woven into the fabric of my life, teaching me the value of perseverance, integrity, and excellence in everything I do.

Many things in life happen without explanation, and I've learned to accept that I may not always understand why. God's ways are higher than ours, often beyond our comprehension. Even when life felt like a tangled mess, I have seen His hand weaving a greater story. His design may not always be clear, but He is always faithful. Each moment, whether joyful or challenging, is a thread He uses to create a masterpiece far more beautiful than I could ever imagine.

PART 1
I Was Totally Unaware of What Was Possible

"But those who hope in the Lord will renew their strength. They will soar on wings like eagles. They will run and not grow weary, they will walk and not be faint."
Isaiah 40:31

CHAPTER 1

Seek and You Shall Find

---

*"It is the glory of God to conceal a matter; to search out a matter
is the glory of kings."*
—*Proverbs 25:2*

The Seeker Will Find

I have always been a seeker, drawn to discovering the deeper truths about life. It's as if God placed a thread of curiosity in my heart, inviting me to unravel life's mysteries and discover His purpose for me. My desire to understand concepts, relationships, and the deeper truths of life has been a constant theme in my journey. It can be a beautiful trait most of the time, but not everyone appreciates it. Some people, bound by fear or traditions, view questions as loose threads that threaten to unravel their sense of stability. But I believe seeking is essential to growth. If you don't understand what you believe, how can you help anyone else understand it? Blindly following may feel comfortable, but it limits you.

I want to encourage anyone who feels compelled to ask questions not to stop. Asking questions can deepen your commitment to God. Life's potential is unlocked when we dare to step outside our comfort zones and challenge what we know, even when those around us prefer the safety of what they already know. Seeking takes courage, especially when the path ahead feels tangled and unclear.

It's through this seeking that you grow closer to God and discover the masterpiece He is weaving in your life.

Humans are the only part of creation that can exist without truly growing. Everything else dies if it isn't thriving. Some people may seem content or even happy to remain where they are, but the sad reality is that without growth, they are stagnant. To be stagnant is to be stuck, with nothing changing or flourishing. It's like a plant that has been watered once and then forgotten; it may survive for a while, but without care, it wilts and eventually dies.

Are we meant to simply survive as Christians, or are we called to thrive? Thriving is about more than existence; it's about living fully in God's design. A thriving person is one who seeks, grows, and allows God to weave their life into a beautiful tapestry. Seeking is a vital part of thriving. Without it, you remain stuck, disconnected from the purpose God has for you.

So I ask: What makes you thrive? What are the characteristics of a person who is truly living? Seeking is the key. It opens the door to discovering what is true, what is real, and what God wants from and for your life. When you keep seeking, you allow God to guide your steps, weaving every thread of your journey into His perfect design.

> *"And without faith it is impossible to please God, because anyone who comes to him must believe that he exists and that he rewards those who earnestly seek him."* *Hebrews 11:6*

What Makes Someone a Seeker?

What makes someone a seeker? Often, it's because life hasn't turned out the way they thought it would. Have you ever wondered if maybe God wants you to be a seeker, but you were taught all your life to simply follow along? It's easy to settle into routines, not realizing there could be so much more for you. Many people default to being followers, shaped by their circumstances, rather than daring to ask for more. I truly believe the kingdom of darkness thrives on complacency. True seekers, however, resist stagnation. They understand that growth comes from asking, searching, and pursuing.

Jesus tells us, "Seek and you shall find" (Matthew 7:7)

How often are you seeking?

In your quest for understanding, you may occasionally lose your way, take a misguided path, or become completely off track. But the beauty of seeking is that God's grace allows you to get back up, redirect your steps, and continue forward. He doesn't leave you stranded in your confusion; He helps you in your searching. Even when the path seems tangled, He is weaving those moments into His greater design for your life.

Having someone to guide and support you in your seeking can make all the difference. While that's not always the case, you're never truly alone if you have Jesus with you. I like to believe that no matter where you are on the journey of life, God is always waiting along the path—ready for you to open your heart and hands to let Him walk with you. He is that good.

Seeking God is foundational to living a meaningful life. The sooner you embrace this truth, the richer your journey becomes. That doesn't mean life will suddenly be perfect or that you'll get everything you've ever dreamed of. I know because I've been there. When I accepted Jesus as my Savior, I thought my life would be without struggles, that I would live perfectly, and that I would always do the right thing. But that was wishful thinking, not truth. It was a diluted version of faith at best, and at worst, a lie the devil used to derail me.

"Indeed, if you call out for insight and cry aloud for understanding, and if you look for it as for silver and search for it as for hidden treasure, then you will understand the fear of the Lord and find the knowledge of God." Proverbs 2:3–5

For years, I stayed busy trying to do everything right, thinking it would bring me closer to God. But all that striving only blinded me to the grace and love that were already mine. The truth is, seeking God isn't about perfection. It's about trusting that His grace will cover your missteps and that His love will guide you forward, weaving every thread of your journey into something beautiful and meaningful.

The Weight of Perfectionism

I wanted to be a Christian. I believed that Jesus died to save me and that I was His child. For years, I measured my faith by works—by how I dressed, what I owned, who I spent time with, what our house looked like, even what kind of vehicle we drove. I convinced myself that these things mattered, that they were a reflection of my righteousness. But beneath it all was a constant battle within to be good enough.

This struggle stayed with me well into my late thirties—sad, but true. When this is how you live, it affects everything. Every thought, every action, is filtered through the lens of doing it right. It becomes a deeply ingrained way of life, a burden that is nearly impossible to lay down. And for a long time, I didn't even realize how much it weighed me down or how deeply it influenced my life.

At some point, I started noticing something: I didn't have joy. My life felt like a repetition of how my parents had lived years before me. I could see it, but I didn't know how to change it. What contributed to my unhappiness was the weight of perfectionism, a theme that will come up more than once in this book—because striving for perfection was a big part of the baggage I carried.

I can remember so many nights going to bed feeling like an absolute failure as a Christian. I was exhausted from trying to live up to impossible standards, always falling short. But change didn't happen overnight. It was gradual—moment by moment, capturing my thoughts, reflecting on what I was thinking and feeling, and allowing God to work in my heart.

I had reached the bottom of the barrel (as the saying goes)—the depths of despair. I was done. And I told the Lord I couldn't do this anymore. If this was what the Christian life was going to be—endless striving, constant guilt, and never feeling like enough—then I didn't want it.

Looking back, that moment wasn't the end; it was the beginning of real transformation. It didn't mean all my struggles disappeared in an instant, but it was the moment I could feel myself surrendering to whatever God had in store for me.

And that surrender didn't just affect my faith—it touched every part of my life, including my marriage. I had spent years carrying unspoken expectations about how things "should" be, believing that if I just did everything right, everything around me would fall into place. But the harder I tried, the more frustrated and disappointed I became. My marriage wasn't as happy as I thought it could be, and if I was honest, much of that came from the pressure I put on myself and the conditions I unknowingly placed on my spouse and family.

But after that moment of surrender, something changed. I still carried struggles, and I didn't have all the answers, but in the months that followed, God began to open doors for me to see a different way of living—one not built on expectations, perfection, or proving myself, but on grace. Slowly, I began to release the need for control. I started letting go of the weight I had placed on my shoulders and on the people I loved.

It took time—lots of time—to unlearn old patterns and let go of the belief that my worth was tied to how well I performed. And even now, I am still a work in progress. But I can say this with certainty: God's grace has been reshaping me, one step at a time.

I was twelve years old when I read a book about a boy who became a Christian, and I remember wanting to be one, too. It sounded so wonderful. I decided that when I turned fourteen, I would give my heart to Jesus, just like the boy in the story. Time went on, and a few months after my fourteenth birthday, I did just that. I was so happy. I felt free, and the world seemed so full of possibility. But it wasn't long before reality set in, and things didn't go the way I thought they would. I struggled with my siblings and felt like a boat with oars but no one to help row. When you're young, having a guiding hand or someone to walk alongside you is so necessary. It can be the one thing that keeps you from giving up.

Don't misunderstand me: my parents cared deeply. They were doing their best in new territory. They believed in Christian living, but the kind they had been shown wasn't filled with joy or fulfillment in the Lord. It was a life of constant striving, hardship, and little room for emotion or affection. My dad, especially, grew up without affirmation or acceptance of self. To him, anything that focused on the self was of the devil. His parents instilled in him a fear of pride, and they weren't entirely wrong. Pride can lead to trouble, and the Bible speaks against it. Proverbs 16:18 reminds us, "Pride goes before destruction, a haughty spirit before a fall." But they took it to an extreme. There is no way we can live well enough through our efforts to prove we don't have pride or other things that come between us and God.

James 4:6 tells us, "God opposes the proud but shows favor to the humble," reminding us that grace, not striving, is what draws us closer to Him. Perhaps understanding this can provide clarity for the deeper struggles I faced growing up.

Our family home wasn't always peaceful. Conflict was common, and unresolved tension created insecurity. A peaceful home requires all parties to work toward the same goal. When that doesn't happen, conflict festers, building walls that make connections difficult. It reminds me of the verse in Ephesians 4:26–27: "Do not let the sun go down while you are still angry, and do not give the devil a foothold." Anger that lingers allows the devil to work his destruction in our lives. Resolving conflict strengthens relationships and leads to abundant living. When you release anger and hold onto forgiveness, you not only heal relationships but also free yourself from the weight of bitterness.

Not all anger is wrong, but anger that leads to sin is. It becomes harmful when it creates division, hinders reconciliation, or makes forgiveness difficult. In my childhood home, the constant striving to live "right" based on someone else's interpretation of God's Word left little room for grace. My parents deeply desired to do what was right, but the weight of expectations in their relationship often left them frustrated and on edge. At the time, I didn't recognize how much those unspoken expectations shaped their interactions. Communication didn't always come easily, and misunderstandings sometimes led to conflict. The pressure to keep up with everything—making a living, raising a family, and balancing spiritual traditions with new ways of doing things—made reconciliation even harder. The demands of daily life left little space for open conversations, and unresolved tension often lingered beneath the surface.

It wasn't until later, as I became more aware of what was happening in my own life, that I realized I was carrying the same pattern. Though my husband and I didn't fight, we didn't always have a strong connection, either. The weight of expectations—spoken and unspoken—still created distance.

Grace is what sets us free. I am so grateful that God, in His grace, gives us opportunities to step out of the cycle of striving and into a new way—one filled with deeper connections, better communication, and the freedom to live in His grace. We don't have to stay stuck in old patterns; He gently leads us toward growth, healing, and life rooted in His love. When we trust in Him, we can release the weight of perfectionism and embrace the peace that comes from resting in His sufficiency.

> *"For by one sacrifice he has made perfect forever those who are being made holy."*   *Hebrews 10:14*

Navigating Identity and Boundaries

My parents believed that each choice made, no matter how small, had the power to define one's righteous standing. However, this definition was often shaped by someone else's interpretation of God's Word. It's why there are so many groups claiming their way is the only right way.

I sometimes wonder, who is truly living the way God intended? Every group teaches their perspective, and when that's what you're raised in, it becomes your reality. In the setting I grew up in, there was often a lingering sense of uncertainty—questions were always present, like *Am I saved? Am I doing enough? Am I living "right"?* These questions aren't inherently bad, but they can overshadow the truth of what Jesus accomplished for us. He came down from heaven to die for our redemption. If we're constantly striving to prove we're enough, what does that say about the work of the cross? True freedom comes from believing and resting in His grace.

My childhood wasn't always negative. My parents taught us valuable lessons—to work hard, to do a job well, and to be responsible. They instilled in us a spirit of generosity and usefulness, traits I'm deeply grateful for. However, as the oldest, I took on more responsibility than I should have. Despite the challenges, there were moments of growth and learning that shaped who I am today. I hated conflict and became a people pleaser, doing whatever I could to keep the peace. It seemed easier to make everyone happy than to risk confrontation.

Trying to please everyone comes with its own troubles. I buried my opinions and tried to be neutral, thinking it was the best way to maintain harmony. In reality, I was burying myself. God gave each of us a mind to think, contribute, and offer solutions. Suppressing your voice to please others isn't living for His purpose. It's being a puppet, pulled by everyone else's expectations.

Learning to set boundaries was a struggle. Saying "no" felt selfish. I believed my only duty was to care for others, and if I did anything for myself, it was wrong. But boundaries are essential for wellness—spiritually, emotionally, mentally, and physically. Jesus didn't call us to be yes-people. He called us to live in balance, understanding when to serve and when to rest. Boundaries are not selfish; they are tools for thriving in His purpose. These tools include clarifying your values and expectations, asking for space when needed, and seeking help without guilt.

Early Struggles and Lessons in Abundance

Learning to set boundaries laid the groundwork for my understanding of what it means to truly thrive in Christ's purpose. However, this lesson was hard-won amidst the challenges of my early years. I worked hard and did what I thought was expected of me for my parents and siblings. Yet there were times I felt confused because our lives didn't match the ideal image I had in my head. I thought Christian families got along well, never argued, and always exuded happiness. That wasn't my experience growing up. Many of my memories from ages twelve to eighteen involve arguments about money, religion, or who was right or wrong. Even the mention of separation—the "D" word—terrified me. What would happen to us if my parents split up?

Years later, someone told me that while my parents' relationship wasn't perfect, their staying together was still a good thing. I've reflected on that, and while I see their perseverance as admirable, part of me still wishes their relationship had been different—filled with more peace and unity. Marriage is meant to be a partnership, a "we're on the same page, I've got your back" kind of bond. When conflict remains unresolved in a home, it leaves lasting effects that eventually demand healing.

Even during the years we homeschooled and attended our home church, there wasn't a sense of joy or fulfillment. It felt like we were just existing. Some might wonder why that wasn't enough. But just living isn't what Jesus calls us to. Where is the abundant life He promised if we're merely surviving? Abundance isn't about material wealth; it's about living in the present, appreciating the good in life, and finding joy even amidst challenges. It means seeking to learn from difficulties and embracing the beauty within them.

I understand now why some people who grow up in religious homes turn away from Christianity. If your experience is filled with conflict, strict rules, and judgment, it's hard to reconcile that with the idea of a loving God. For me, life didn't match what I thought it was supposed to be. Maybe I lived too much in an idealistic fantasy. I'm learning to extend grace to myself and others. Life isn't perfect, and conflict is inevitable. What matters is how we address it.

Our little church group eventually dissolved. The two families who had been with us decided to leave and join a larger group. All of us children had gone to school together until they left. One year, we had an outsider as our teacher; the next, my dad taught us; and the final year, my uncle took on the role. The families who left were clearly seeking something better, and perhaps they found it. I don't really know why my dad didn't follow their path. I have vague memories of him and my mom discussing people who had left the church and their struggles.

After those families left, we started attending the church connected to my dad's relatives. It was a very conservative group with plain clothing and basic vehicles. This shift brought its own set of challenges, but it became part of the tapestry of my upbringing, one that God continues to weave into His purpose for my life.

Navigating Two Worlds: A Journey of Belonging

This church was the one my grandfather had belonged to when Dad was young. It was the church they went to before moving to Paraguay. I had lots of cousins there, and we enjoyed being with them. However, I remember feeling like I didn't belong there, either. They were a group of people who believed a little differently than we did. Their homes were very plain, their clothes even plainer, and their vehicles were basic models, some painted uniformly in a single color. This simplicity was their way of living right.

Since our little group had parted ways, we needed somewhere to go to school. Public school wasn't an option. Dad asked if we could attend the one-room school in this group, and he also inquired about us attending the Holdeman group school. The Holdeman group responded before the others, so we started attending their school.

Being at this school, surrounded by people whose beliefs and practices differed from ours, wasn't easy. We stood out. Most of them were kind, but there were those who made it clear they saw us as different and out of place. And it was true: we were different. Their homes were fancier, the ladies wore dresses with printed flowers, and they drove nice cars. Everything they had seemed a notch above what I was familiar with, at least from what I could tell.

Between the two groups, I didn't feel like I belonged anywhere. We were navigating two different worlds. Dad's teachings emphasized simplicity: no printed clothes, solid colors only, no short sleeves, no short dresses. Anything else would have been considered scandalous. Everything we owned had to be simple and plain. This would be one instance of extreme. Yet, there was a deep longing in my heart to belong somewhere. Looking back, I see how this longing was a thread woven through every part of my life, pulling me toward connections and meaning in ways I couldn't fully understand at the time.

Our lives were quiet and unremarkable. Dad worked hard, Mom worked hard, and we children did what we could. I can appreciate that my parents took time to make memories around family gatherings and holidays. Thanksgiving meals were special, often shared with extended family. As I got older, I did much of the cooking. I enjoyed creating recipes and seeing how everyone relished my efforts. Cooking became one of my happy places. It was like adding vibrant threads to our family's tapestry, a way to contribute something meaningful and beautiful to our daily lives.

Occasional outings were highlights in our week. After church on Sundays, Dad would sometimes buy food from McDonald's or KFC, and we'd have a picnic at the park. Buying fast food was special. I remember trying to replicate the KFC slaw. It turned out close to the same flavor. I'm not sure how often we did this, but I remember feeling happy doing something different. Those moments, though simple, felt like golden threads weaving joy and connection into the fabric of our family.

I attended the Holdeman school for two years, completing my seventh and eighth grades there. Even with some friends and people who showed interest in me, I still struggled to feel like I truly belonged. From age fourteen to eighteen, I spent most of my time at home, helping Dad with some of his jobs. The summer I was sixteen, Mom went to Paraguay for about a month, leaving me in charge. That was a pivotal moment for me. It was a time when I began to see the value of responsibility and independence, threads that would later strengthen my sense of self.

When I turned eighteen, I got my driver's license and a job at a dry cleaner's. The job lasted only two weeks. Looking back, I think Dad worried I was becoming too independent, and maybe I was. Until I turned twenty, I didn't do much on my own. That was the approved age when I could make my own decisions. In the Bible, twenty years old is considered adulthood—the age to take part in entering the Promised Land. I believe this influenced Dad's perspective on when independence was acceptable. It's interesting to think about how cultural and spiritual threads from generations before us continue to shape the fabric of our lives.

I was okay with this system at the time, but I was still searching and wondering what I needed to do with my life.

Seeking to Belong

I did go out with some cousins for social activities. Every once in a while, I would go to a little diner in the evening for supper. I worked for Dad until they moved to Tennessee. My life didn't have a lot of excitement. That all changed when I decided to get baptized.

I stayed in Mississippi because I decided to join the Holdeman Mennonite church. I was baptized on August 15, 1999. It was the beginning of feeling like maybe I had found my place to belong. This decision felt like weaving a new thread into my life, one of commitment and connection to a community, even as I continued to navigate my sense of truly belonging.

In the meantime, I began my teaching career at the old one-room school, the same school I had attended for three years, the same school my dad went to when he was young. I taught there for about three months. The reason it didn't last any longer was that I was accused of encouraging the students to be daring. I wasn't, but that's what some of the parents implied. "Daring" may not be quite the right word, but it taught me an important lesson. Looking back, I realize people are often afraid of things that differ from what they're used to. If something is different, it's seen as something to fear. While caution has its place, being open is essential. Let us not be like the Pharisees, who, blinded by self-righteousness, failed to recognize the truth of the Messiah before their eyes.

What if I ask the questions? What if I believe and trust that God will not let me down?

I loved those children and felt they needed fresh perspectives to open their minds, but it wasn't their time, and it wasn't for me to show them. I like to believe the students have good memories of those few short months together. I see those moments as small but significant threads in their lives and mine.

During this time, I had a friend I would visit at her workplace nearby. She was an amazing listener and often provided valuable insights. Connections like these are so important. Jesus had His inner circle of friends, and we need those kinds of friendships, too. They can be your sounding board, offer guidance, or pick you up when you fall. I am grateful for those relationships that stood by me during challenging times. Friendships, I've come to learn, are golden threads, bright and enduring parts of life's tapestry.

It was such an odd time in my life. I stayed at a friend's house for about two weeks, then lived in our old house until I took a teaching position in Leland in January. Life has its twists and turns, but perspective plays a huge part in how well it goes for you. Life is challenging, but it is also beautiful. Every twist and turn adds a new dimension to the story being woven.

The teaching position in Leland lasted until the school year ended. I stayed the summer there, working for a man who owned a cabinet shop and later became my uncle. It was a good job with an excellent boss. After summer ended, I left to teach in Sharon Springs, Kansas. It was a small place with few people. While the community was kind, there weren't many youths to connect with. My best friend was teaching in a neighboring congregation, and we'd travel together to meet new friends at other congregations. I'm grateful we could share those adventures.

Friendships are important to me, and I work hard to maintain close connections. There are times in the busyness of life when I lose touch with someone, but I am always amazed at how it doesn't take much time to feel like it was just yesterday that we last talked. True friendships stand the test of time, offering the ability to reconnect quickly, no matter how long it's been. Cultivating relationships that help you thrive in your journey of seeking and learning is vital. These connections are golden threads in life's tapestry, essential to growth, strength, and resilience.

Seeking and Self-Education

Seeking God in our daily lives has to become a practice. I read a lot when I was younger; I still do. Learning and understanding how things work or how I can be a better person have been part of my journey. I don't think I realized how deep that desire to be the kind of person that would honor God and be who He wanted me to be was within me.

> *"You will seek me and find me when you seek me with all your heart."*   Jeremiah 29:13

The journey of growing and learning is ever-changing. Life brings lots of challenges, but they are also lessons, and you have to face them or be overcome by them. Every lesson is another thread, a chance to add to the richness and complexity of the tapestry. You may not see the beauty in it yet, but God does. He is the master weaver, after all.

My formal education was limited to 8th grade in a private school. My mom wanted me to receive my GED, which I accomplished. I also took an accounting course and graduated from that. While I don't use it much, it's a reminder of how much I enjoy learning. Education doesn't have to come from prestigious schools; today, we have nearly limitless access to knowledge. However, learning is only valuable when it's applied—otherwise, it's wasted potential. Scripture reminds us that the most important pursuits are not about amassing knowledge but living in obedience to God:

> *"And what does the Lord require of you? To act justly and to love mercy and to walk humbly with your God."*   Micah 6:8

I've come to realize that true education shapes your character, drawing you closer to God and helping you live out His purpose. It's not just about acquiring skills but about growing into someone who honors and serves Him wholeheartedly.

As you come to the end of this chapter and gauge your seeking level, I hope wherever you find yourself, whether it is a new thought or something you have been at for many years, you give yourself lots of grace. Seeking isn't for the faint of heart; it takes courage and a willingness to mess up. Don't judge yourself for whatever state you are in at this moment.

As you consider these questions, be honest with yourself and remember, it's not about being wrong or right. It is about being willing to change and grow.

Reflection Questions:

1. What threads of curiosity or longing has God placed in your heart?
2. Are there areas of your life that feel frayed or tangled? How might God be weaving those into His purpose?
3. How can you seek God more intentionally in your daily life?

CHAPTER 2

Covered by His Grace

"Out of his fullness, we have all received grace in place of grace already given."
—John 1:16

God's Constant Presence

Looking back over the years, I can see now how God was always with me. I like to believe I felt His presence in the middle of my daily life, even when I didn't fully understand it. His nearness was constant, even when I was unaware. I desired to serve Him, and I believe He blessed that desire by staying close to me, walking with me through every season.

Despite my inability to fully grasp His presence, I can now see how God was directing events in my life to guide me and teach me. Whether it was a moment of unexpected peace in the middle of chaos, a word of encouragement from someone when I needed it most, or a solution to a problem I couldn't see my way through, His hand was always there, carefully weaving together the threads of my life.

These moments were often subtle and easy to overlook, like delicate stitches in a tapestry, but they laid a foundation of faith and trust in His constant care. Looking back, I realize that even in my most uncertain times, God's presence was a steady anchor, holding me in place and quietly shaping me for the journey ahead. Often, His reassurance would come in unexpected ways—a phrase from a song, a quote that spoke directly to what I was dealing with, or a conversation with a friend that felt perfectly timed. In those moments, I could sense that God was near, reminding me that I wasn't alone.

But there was one struggle in particular that weighed on me. Just recently, I feel like He did some deep work in my heart. There were times when I wondered if I would ever get through it, if I would ever feel peace about it. Six months ago, I probably would have told you that I didn't know if I'd ever get to the other side of this. Yet here I am—changed.

God didn't remove the struggle overnight, but He helped me through people, through conversations, and through slow and steady processes that reshaped my heart and mind. Maybe it was a word of encouragement at just the right time. Maybe it was the willingness to sit with my feelings instead of running from them. Maybe it was realizing that I didn't have to carry it all alone. I can't pinpoint just one moment when everything shifted, but I can say this: God was working, even when I couldn't see it. And now, standing on the other side, I feel peace.

The situation hasn't necessarily changed, but I have. And that's what makes all the difference.

The Burden of Expectations

Life, however, was challenging. Not because I had a horrible childhood or was mistreated, but because I placed such high expectations on myself and others. While my parents provided well for my physical needs, ensuring I always had food and clothing, I often felt neglected in terms of emotional support and loving affirmation. The absence of that nurturing connection left a void that shaped how I approached relationships and life. I made life harder than it needed to be by trying to compensate for what I lacked, often focusing on achieving perfection rather than embracing grace.

I know my parents loved me, but they didn't always show it in ways that I felt. Affection is vital to a child's well-being. It reassures them that they matter and that someone truly has their best interest at heart. Growing up, there were so many things I had to figure out on my own. Yet even in those moments, I believe God was with me. He gave me a sense of guidance, helping me discern right from wrong so I could make choices I wouldn't regret.

I longed for God to be my friend, my source of strength, and the one I depended on. But I didn't know how to cultivate that kind of relationship. I prayed to Him, believed in Him, and trusted that He heard my prayers. I never doubted His existence, yet I misunderstood the depths of His care for me. Likewise, I didn't fully grasp how invested He was in my life and my struggles. How He wanted to weave the beautiful and even the not-so-beautiful threads of my life. He knew I would have some tangled threads that would take time to untangle, like understanding how much He longed for me to accept His wonderful grace.

Misunderstanding Grace

As time went on, I unknowingly adopted the wrong concept of God. Without realizing it, I began living as though I had to prove my worth to Him. My life became a cycle of trying to earn His love, striving for perfection, and believing I had to perform to stay in His good graces. I'd lost sight of the truth of His unconditional love and everlasting grace.

This mindset convinced me that to be worthy of God's love, I had to perform flawlessly—all the time. And when I inevitably fell short, I felt unworthy. The weight of this belief was crushing, leaving me feeling like a failure in every area of my life. It was a hard and heavy burden to carry.

In my striving, I often found myself discouraged. I could never measure up to the ideals I held. But where did those ideals come from? Who gave me the notion that I had to be perfect? They came from the things I heard and how I interpreted them. These expectations became like tangled threads, binding me to a life of frustration and disappointment.

I lived for too many years as a Christian in a state of performing, striving, digging, and trying to do what I thought was required to be right. I believed that if I worked hard enough, prayed long enough, and followed every perceived expectation, then maybe I would finally feel worthy.

There is nothing wrong with striving when it is for things that will change and improve our lives. Sometimes, digging is necessary to get to the root of our problems. But it must be the kind of digging that makes a difference, not the kind that only magnifies what's wrong and leaves you more discouraged than before.

For years, I didn't realize I was caught in a cycle of religious striving. I thought I was doing it all for God, but deep down, I was trying to prove something—maybe to myself, maybe to others, maybe even to God. And yet, no matter how much I did, it never felt like enough. I wasn't feeling closer to Him. If anything, I felt more distant. I was exhausted, empty, and wondering why all my efforts weren't leading to the peace and joy I had been promised.

Looking back, I can't say there was one exact moment when everything changed. It wasn't as though a switch flipped overnight. Instead, the transformation happened gradually, like a slow unraveling of the beliefs I had clung to for so long. But I do remember a turning point—after that weekend retreat, something in me shifted.

I left with a deep longing to be truly grounded in God, not just to go through the motions of faith, but to actually live in it.

That desire led me on a journey. Slowly, I began to question what I had been chasing. I started to ask myself if all my striving was really for God's glory—or if it was about proving something. That realization came like a gentle whisper at first, but over time, it grew louder: I had been striving for something that was already mine.

As I continued to seek God, I began to realize that His truth was the only thing that truly mattered. It's not that everything else— the struggles, the expectations, the weight of trying to measure up—didn't matter at all, but in the long view of living for God, I knew I was going to be okay. My striving didn't define me. My failures didn't disqualify me. What mattered was His grace, His love, and His truth. And in that, I could finally rest.

You can stop striving, too. You can accept that there is grace— grace that covers you completely. Not because you earned it, but because it was never yours to earn in the first place.

As a young person, I often thought about the future. I didn't want to look back and wish I'd done things differently. Even back then, I had this desire to live without regrets. It is the theme of my life now, but I mess up even now.

Still, there were lessons I missed back then, things I wish I had understood better. But I could only act on what I knew and understood at the time. Life, after all, is a journey of continual learning if you pay attention.

The Lies of Perfectionism

When I made the decision to follow Christ, to believe in Jesus, and to place my hope in Him, life began to change. I remember feeling joy, a sense of freedom, and a newfound purpose. But the sad truth is that feeling didn't last long. I wish someone had told me then that I didn't need to live by a set of man-made rules to stay in God's grace. Instead, I needed to seek His Word and live by His truth. But I didn't know that at the time. So, I did what I thought was right—I added expectations and rules, thinking they would make me a better Christian. The weight of striving to be perfect became exhausting, but I convinced myself that this was what God required. And if you've ever tried to be perfect, you know how futile it is.

Maybe you've experienced something similar—starting with something good, something true, but then slowly adding layers to it, complicating what was meant to be simple. That's exactly what happened to me. My journey with Christ started in faith, but over time, I twisted it into something that turned into an endless cycle of striving. It became about my version of the gospel, rather than the one Jesus had already given me. And I wasn't happy. It pains me to admit that I lived on the outskirts of God's unconditional love and grace for too many years—believing in it but not fully embracing it. I made faith harder than it needed to be. But when the truth finally settled in my heart—when I began stripping away the weight of expectations and adding only the layers of His truth—everything changed. I no longer strive to be perfect. I am free.

I often felt I could never be truly good enough. I don't know why I believed I had to be perfect before God could love me, but those were the requirements I thought I had to meet. I wasn't worthy unless I did everything right. How I longed to feel good enough—to be worthy to be called His child, to feel like I deserved His love. This deep longing often left me ending my days filled with lingering disappointment, believing I had failed yet again to present myself as worthy.

As I reflect on the many moments over the years, I can now see how God was trying to tell me that He loved me deeply and unconditionally. It is a truth that is finally beginning to settle deep in my heart, weaving its way into every corner of my being, reminding me that His grace has always been enough.

I often felt like I was in a dark room filled with high bars that I could never reach. These bars, meant to be climbed to attain something greater, were always just out of reach, taunting me with their impossibility. It was discouraging. Every bar in that room seemed unreachable by my standards. Why couldn't there have been some lower ones, ones that would give me a sense of possibility and hope?

Instead, I always felt like I had missed yet another opportunity to attain worthiness. Oh, the burdens we bring upon ourselves in the name of religion and righteousness! And let me tell you, I did bring heavy burdens upon myself; heavy burdens of having an immaculate house, and I was to be available at all times for all people.

What breaks my heart is how those burdens spilled over onto my family. For them, they had to be well-behaved children, and my husband was supposed to be and act a certain way. It saddens me to reflect on how those expectations affected them, but what truly matters now is that I've learned. I can do better—so much better—and by God's grace, I am doing better.

It had been a never-ending cycle: try and fail, try and fail. God knows how much I tried. I couldn't see an end in sight for the striving and the weight I carried. When you begin to realize and accept that the truth of God's love is not dependent on your performance, you will be free indeed. His grace is not earned; it is given freely.

Breaking Free from Perfectionism

Perfection is a lie, one crafted by the enemy to keep us in bondage. Trying to live perfectly is exhausting, a relentless cycle of striving that brings nothing but frustration. The lies of perfection keep us so busy that we miss the true joy and freedom God intends for us. Satan uses this illusion of perfection to distract us from the real power that comes from leaning on Jesus and His promises.

> *"Be perfect, therefore, as your heavenly Father is perfect."*   *Matthew 5:48*

This verse speaks of being perfect, but I don't believe it implies that we will achieve perfection in ourselves. Jesus is the only One who is perfect, and our perfection comes through Him. The call to perfection is an invitation to lean fully on Christ, whose righteousness covers us.

If Satan can keep us preoccupied with trying to be perfect, we will miss out on the abundant life Jesus offers. We know that Jesus died for us, but we fail to live within the joy and peace that His sacrifice brings. The joy and peace of being loved not because of what we do, but because of who we are.

There are Scriptures that call us to be perfect, to be holy, and to offer ourselves as living sacrifices to God: "Therefore, I urge you, brothers and sisters, in view of God's mercy, to offer your bodies as a living sacrifice, holy and pleasing to God—this is your true and proper worship" (Romans 12:1). I internalized these verses in a way that led me to believe I couldn't be acceptable to God until I became this perfect person, doing everything right. I began to question: What does it mean to do the "right thing"? What is the right way to dress, to talk, to live? Who decides what is right? Is it God, or is it an idea created by man?

When I first became a Christian, I didn't have these ideas in my head. They grew over time as I listened to sermons, heard others speak, and absorbed teachings influenced by human interpretations of faith. My upbringing and the expectations of what a true Christian was, I can see now, created a life of endless striving. I built a facade, smiling and portraying everything was fine, while inside, I was burdened with confusion and feeling unworthy. I couldn't let anyone know what was really going on inside me. It was not pretty. I just knew that if they knew how it was, I would be a complete failure in their eyes.

I've observed that people often identify problems and stop there; they uncover the issue but don't seek solutions. This can feel defeating, but it's often because the problem surpasses their knowledge or ability to address it. It's frustrating to encounter this, but here is hope: God knows every limitation we face. He knows who will help us take the next step. Even when you feel alone, don't give up hope—there is help on the other side of your problems. Solutions exist, though they may not come in the way you expect. We must keep an open mind and also understand that help may be from the most unexpected sources.

Let go of trying to be perfect. Remember, perfection isn't required because Jesus is our perfection. As Christians, our duty is to obey and to continually grow and learn. Each day, we are either becoming more of who we're meant to be or remaining stuck. I've chosen to reject being stuck. Life is hard enough without adding unnecessary burdens. If you feel stuck, don't believe it's permanent. There is a way out, with God's help.

Grace in Motherhood and Marriage

After getting married and having children, those unattainable bars felt even more unreachable. When I prayed, all I could focus on was asking for forgiveness for the ways I had fallen short that day. Gratitude was absent from my prayers, replaced by a fixation on my perceived failures. What I know now is that bringing gratitude into your prayer life changes everything. God weaves the good things into your life, and when you thread your prayers with gratitude, it will bring out the beautiful parts in your life.

I longed to be kind and loving, but more often than not, I found myself frustrated and impatient with everyone around me. At the time, I didn't fully understand why. Now, I can see that those feelings weren't a reflection of me being inherently bad or unloving—they were the result of carrying the weight of performance in the name of being the "right kind" of Christian.

So much of my impatience and frustration came from living in reaction mode. I never stopped to ask myself why I was feeling the way I was—I just responded. My mind was often weighed down with worries, responsibilities, and unspoken pressures, and without realizing it, I would lash out at my children. It had nothing to do with them, yet they bore the brunt of my overwhelm.

I didn't know how to pause, take a breath, and ask myself what was really going on. Instead, I kept pushing forward, trying to meet expectations I had placed on myself—expectations I thought defined what it meant to be a good wife, a good mom, a good Christian. But that striving only left me depleted, short-tempered, and disconnected from the grace I so desperately needed.

If we were late for church, I felt like a bad Christian. If I raised my voice to my children, I believed I was a horrible mother. If I had a negative thought about someone, I felt unworthy to be called a Christian because a "true" Christian wouldn't think such things. While I do believe in striving to live a kind and good life, the immense pressure I placed on myself to perform perfectly was detrimental. It caused far more harm than good, creating a cycle of shame and self-doubt.

My mothering wasn't what I hoped it would be, and my marriage often felt like it fell short of the ideal. I felt alone so much of the time. I believed I was the only one who had problems, and that no one could think well of me if they knew how flawed I really was. So I hid behind busyness, always saying "yes" to any requests made of me. I was afraid that if people saw the real me, they wouldn't love me. I didn't have a safe space to share my struggles without being labeled. I didn't understand how deeply that fear of being one of "those people" affected me.

But even then, God was preparing a way for me. He placed a friend in my life—someone I could confide in, someone who could listen to my deepest fears and worries. Looking back, I see how God was working behind the scenes, setting the foundation for a friendship that would become a lifeline. God often works in ways we can't see, and only later do we realize His plan. He is constantly weaving the threads of our lives, creating beauty from the frayed parts, the parts we wonder if there is any beauty left. But God, with grace, can create something beautiful.

Discovering the Depth of Grace

God has been present in my life from the moment I first understood Him as someone to know and believe in. Yet it's only in recent years that I've started to grasp the magnitude of His grace and love. To be covered by His grace is not just a spiritual concept—it is a life-transforming reality. God's grace is a profound gift, a divine shelter, and a reminder of His unwavering and unconditional love.

When we dwell within the realm of His grace, life becomes abundant, rich with purpose, and filled with peace. Life will still have its struggles, and at times, you may find it not so peaceful. But God's love is encompassing, and it's Jesus who unlocks our ability to fully live under this covering. Jesus came so that we could experience God's grace and love without limits, a covering that extends to every aspect of our lives.

The truth about this grace is woven throughout God's Word. It's there for us to discover, embrace, and build our lives upon. When we seek His truth, it finds us; when we open ourselves to it, it transforms us. God's grace isn't something to be earned—it's a gift freely given, unmerited and overflowing.

Living under His grace means letting go of the exhausting cycle of striving and embracing the rest and assurance found in Him. It's about knowing that His love covers every fault, failure, and inadequacy. In this truth, we find freedom. We are covered by His grace, and in that covering, we are enough.

Let this truth take root in your heart: His grace is sufficient, and His love is unfailing. He's not asking you to prove your worth; He's inviting you to rest in His grace, to trust in His love, and to walk confidently in His promises. You are covered, fully, deeply, and eternally, by His grace.

Extending Grace to Others

I still struggle with extending grace to everyone. Sometimes, my expectations of others hinder me from giving grace. I pray to continue growing in love for others' souls and to extend grace as Jesus did for me. I may never fully understand grace's depth, but I hope that each day I learn more about how to give grace to myself and others.

The fear of being labeled is what keeps many of us from sharing our deepest struggles. We are afraid of being misjudged, of not being enough, and of losing our sense of belonging if others truly knew what we were facing. So, we hide behind shame and guilt, convinced that staying silent is safer than being seen.

Labeling is a subtle undercurrent in my close-knit community. Most of the time, it isn't meant to be malicious—it's simply part of life in a place where people seem to know what everyone is doing. Conversations turn into assumptions, and assumptions turn into quiet judgments. I don't believe people always mean harm, but I do know that this is not what God wants.

I still battle with the weight of labels, both the ones I have carried and the ones I am tempted to place on others. But God is teaching me. In the moments when I feel the pull to judge or categorize someone, He gently whispers to my heart, "Is this how you want to respond? Is it your job to label?"

And I know the answer.

His grace reminds me to extend grace—to let go of my own judgments and to see people the way Jesus sees them. If I want to live in the freedom of His grace, I must also offer that same grace to others. Labels confine people, but grace sets them free.

Jesus never saw people through the lens of their failures or reputations. He saw beyond the labels the world had placed on them. The woman at the well was not just a Samaritan with a broken past—she was someone He called into redemption. Zacchaeus wasn't just a dishonest tax collector—he was someone worth dining with. Paul wasn't just a persecutor of Christians—he was a chosen instrument for the gospel.

When I remember that, I realize how much I need to surrender my own tendency to label and instead choose grace. Because grace is beautiful, and through Him, I can strive to live it out in my relationships, just as He so freely gives it to me.

Paul talks about striving and *contending for the faith* (Jude 1:3), but the kind of striving I once pursued was different. It was rooted in proving myself and in meeting impossible standards. While I was busy trying to uphold an impossible standard, I also had those expectations for others.

Ask yourself, "What am I trying to prove? Who am I trying to be?" I've learned that striving to fit in or live up to others' expectations only brings bondage and a hurting, lonely heart. It makes it hard to love other people well if I have unrealistic expectations for them. This came home to me so clearly after a conversation with my husband about why people do the things they do. When I have these expectations, I am creating a struggle for myself, and it only gets magnified as I add to these expectations.

I need the reminder in Romans 5:8 that says, "But God demonstrates his own love for us in this: While we were still sinners, Christ died for us." This verse has become a cornerstone of my faith. It reminds me that God's love for us existed even when we were separated from Him by sin. Letting that truth sink in has transformed my understanding of grace and acceptance. It's a powerful reminder of the unshakable love God has for each of us, no matter how many times we fall short. This means everyone in my life has this grace waiting for them.

Grace for Every Moment

Grace covers the wrongs in your life, both the mistakes you make and those made by others. Grace is for everyone. When you accept this grace, you'll naturally want to extend it to others. Grace is part of the beautiful gift of salvation Jesus offers.

I used to pray only for forgiveness, focusing solely on the wrongs in my life and the ways I had fallen short. In doing so, I often missed the blessing of recognizing all the good, the ways God was present and working behind the scenes, even in my struggles. That perspective has changed. Now I see that there is grace not only to overcome but also to grow, to become better, and to live more fully in His purpose. I am so deeply grateful for grace. It is truly a blessing and a gift, undeserved, yet freely given. Oh, to not take it for granted! To treasure it, hold on to it, and yet hold it loosely, because grace is not just for me. It is for everyone, meant to be shared and extended as freely as it has been given to me.

Take time to see the good in your life, not just the bad or the things you're doing wrong. Too often, our culture focuses solely on flaws instead of celebrating what God is doing right in us. Jesus came to free us from the bondage of sin. His love propelled Him to willingly endure the cross. While it wasn't easy, His great love for us made Him follow through.

His love and grace do not give us a license to sin, but they cover our imperfections. Jesus died so we could be free, and now God sees us through Jesus. We are covered by His grace, a beautiful and wonderful gift. Grace enables us to love others well and to become who God sees us to be. There is a beautiful hymn about grace, *Grace Greater than Our Sin*. The refrain is so wonderful!

> Grace, grace, God's grace,
>
> Grace that will pardon and cleanse within;
>
> Grace, grace, God's grace,
>
> Grace that is greater than all our sin[1]

Grace keeps us out of judgment and criticism. I'm grateful to have learned that God's grace is all-encompassing, covering far more than I once allowed it to. Jesus never asked me to be perfect before coming to Him; I imposed that expectation on myself. When He died, the veil was torn, removing the separation between us and God. Now, through Jesus, we can approach God freely.

To grow and learn and to keep moving forward is my daily endeavor. I don't expect perfection now; instead, I accept that there is

---

1 Johnston, Julia H. *Grace Greater Than Our Sin.* 1910. Music by Daniel B. Towner.

grace for me to make mistakes and to learn from them. God knew all the things that would cause me problems and made a way for me to learn and understand. He knew that life would be hard, that my confusion and self-imposed expectations would weigh on me, and He prepared a way for me to grow through it all. God saw it all and by His wonderful grace, he is making a way. He will do the same for you.

Why did it have to be that way? I may never know, and I am learning to be at peace with that. The challenges I faced have shaped me into the person I am today. I can take the good, learn from the bad, and grow into someone even more useful for His purpose. We are all being woven into His plan, a tapestry far greater than we can see. I believe each of us is here for a reason: His reason.

But what about those who aren't living to their full potential, or who are weighed down by the heavy burden of striving to be "good enough"? God can still use them. We need to stop underestimating how God can work through people and circumstances, even in ways we don't expect or understand, to fulfill His purpose.

This isn't to say that God forces people to act against their will. Instead, I believe He uses willing and obedient hearts, those who are seeking Him and surrendering to His will. Yet, even when we falter, His grace is sufficient, and His plans remain unshaken. He can redeem any situation, using it for His glory and for our good.

Every step of our journey is filled with choices to move toward or away from His purpose. He provides what we need along the way, but it's up to us to follow through. God works with people whom we may sometimes doubt will meet our expectations of how they should be.

Scriptures are full of stories of people who messed up royally, but God still used them. Here are some of the most intriguing ones to me. Jacob was a deceiver from the beginning, and God still chose to use him. Despite his manipulative ways, he became the father of the twelve tribes of Israel. He learned some hard lessons along the way, but it took years before everything truly connected for him. His story reminds me that God is patient, working through our messiness and mistakes to shape us into who He intends us to be.

Then there's Tamar. She wanted to do what was required of her, but she was neglected by her father-in-law. Left without options, she took extreme measures because, in that culture, a woman without children was considered nothing. And yet, she became part of Jesus' lineage—a powerful testament to God's redemption. Even in the most complicated and broken situations, He can bring beauty and purpose.

And then there's David—oh my, what a man who went to such extreme lengths to cover his sin! He carefully calculated every step, thinking he could get away with it. For someone who had walked so closely with God, it's sobering to see how easily he was overtaken by his own desires. His story is a warning that none of us is immune to temptation. It reminds me that staying close to the source—staying grounded in God—is the key to staying true.

Peter's story is just as striking. He had boldly declared his loyalty to Jesus, yet in a moment of fear, he denied Him—not once, but three times! I can only imagine the shame and guilt he must have felt. But then, Jesus restored him. He didn't cast Peter aside; instead, He reaffirmed His purpose for him. What a picture of grace.

And the list goes on—Moses, who doubted his ability to lead. Paul, who once persecuted Christians before becoming one of the greatest evangelists of all time. Over and over again, the Bible reminds us that God doesn't call the perfect. He redeems the broken, the flawed, and the unworthy.

If He could use them, surely He can use us too. His grace is there for everyone.

Moving Forward in Grace

Learning and growing are lifelong journeys. Growth offers possibilities that are positive, beautiful, and life-giving. Every experience shapes who you are. You can choose to let those experiences help or hinder you; the choice is yours. Embrace grace and keep moving forward on this amazing journey of growth and potential.

Remember, you are covered by His love and grace. Solutions exist, and sometimes you may need to try something new. If staying stuck isn't an option, being uncomfortable may be necessary to move forward. Stepping out of our comfort zone is a challenge, but you must weigh out what you want in your life. Will it be worth it if you find a way to live more alive and vibrant? If you want to know my answer, it is a resounding, "Yes!"

With God, there is always a way, and there is always grace, and with God, all things are possible.

Reflection Questions:

1. How can you embrace God's grace more fully in your life and let go of unrealistic expectations?

2. In what ways can you extend grace to others, especially when they fall short of your expectations?

3. What steps can you take today to focus on the good in your life and see how God is working behind the scenes?

CHAPTER 3

Behind Every Tear, God is There

*"There was no need to be ashamed of tears, for tears bore witness
that a man had the greatest of courage, the courage to suffer."[2]*
—*Viktor E. Frankl*

God Sees Every Tear

This morning, as I prayed for friends navigating difficult times,
tears welled up in my eyes. Life is filled with pain and heartbreak,
and it often leads us to question the goodness of the world. Why is
it so hard? Why do people hurt one another? Where is the justice in
all this chaos? Where is God?

I remember a particularly difficult season in my life when I felt
completely unseen and overwhelmed. I was experiencing a crisis
of faith and wondering where I was in the scheme of life, and as I
knelt there, the weight of it all came pressing down. Tears streamed
down my face, and I cried out to God, asking if He even cared. In
that moment, a deep sense of peace washed over me, as if God was
whispering, "I see you. I'm here. I am your Father." Each tear we
shed matters to Him.

---

2   Frankl, Viktor E. *Man's Search for Meaning*. Translated by Ilse Lasch, Beacon Press, 2006.

"You keep track of all my sorrows. You have collected all my tears in your bottle. You have recorded each one in your book." Psalm 56:8, NLT

This verse comforts me because it reminds me that my tears and your tears are never wasted. They are seen, cherished, and understood by a loving God. It's another moment in time where God once again was weaving the golden threads of love in with the dark threads of pain. That experience opened some doors for me to start a journey of healing like none other.

It was a season where I knew if He didn't help me, no one could. And God in his loving mercy made a way. The journey of new beginnings and changes has been profoundly meaningful. It was another proof that God hears our desperate cries and He sees our tears.

Wrestling with Loving Others Well

I often find myself wrestling with my shortcomings, especially in loving others well. I want to be kind, patient, and gracious, but I fall short more often than I'd like to admit. Why do I struggle to extend love to certain people? Why does forgiveness feel like such a mountain to climb? I've wondered if this is my thorn, the kind of burden Paul describes in the Bible. Recently, I had a moment of reflection about this topic. I could think of it as a thorn in my side, or I could realize that I was just clinging to something. This something was hindering the work God could do in my heart if I were willing. Once you become willing, there is a way. There are times that it is a trial you may have to carry, but God will help you.

It's humbling to confront our weaknesses, but it's also where God's grace meets us. "My grace is sufficient for you, for my power is made perfect in weakness" (2 Corinthians 12:9). This truth reassures me that God doesn't expect perfection; He expects surrender.

Growth isn't instantaneous; it's a slow and sometimes painful process, and tears often accompany it. Yet, through it all, God remains steadfast.

With deep gratitude, I stand in awe of God and how much He loves us and wants to help us to be the best we can be. He truly loves me so well. I know that when your heart is open and ready to receive the help He has to offer, He does not fail to deliver.

Letting Go of Perfection

For so long, I chased perfection (I talk about perfection a lot in this book). It was an intense struggle for me. I wanted to be the perfect wife, mother, friend, and believer. But no matter how hard I tried, I always fell short. I've learned that perfection is a burden we were never meant to carry. God doesn't ask for perfection; He asks for faithfulness.

If you've been striving for an unattainable ideal, it's time to let it go. There's no room for perfection in the beautiful, messy reality of life. Instead, focus on growth, even if it's imperfect and slow. Growth is what you want to use to determine how well you are doing. It's not about competition or comparison. The only comparison you need to make is how well you are doing every day forward. You will never be perfect by your own strength or merit. Your perfection is found in Jesus. It is through Him that you are made complete.

> *"Not that I have already obtained all this, or have already arrived at my goal, but I press on to take hold of that for which Christ Jesus took hold of me."*
> *Philippians 3:12*

Remember that growth, however small, is still progress. The tears you shed through the work you're doing matter to God. All of them, tears of frustration, heartache, sadness, and repentance, are seen by Him. Tears are a language that God understands.

The Sacred Language of Tears

Tears speak a language that words often fail to capture. They convey joy, pain, frustration, and hope. Tears are a sacred expression of the soul's deepest emotions. God, in His infinite understanding, comprehends every tear that falls, even when we feel misunderstood by those around us: "The Lord is close to the brokenhearted; he rescues those whose spirits are crushed" (Psalm 34:18, NLT).

In my younger years, I was ashamed of my tears. I would cry, but no tears would come. It was as if the well that held my tears had run completely dry. One day, that well finally opened, and since then, I have shed tears, but often with a sense of shame lingering in the background.

I had internalized the message that crying was a sign of weakness, something to be hidden away. But as I've grown, I've come to see tears as a gift, a way to release the emotions that weigh heavily on our hearts. Don't keep your emotions bottled up. Tears can serve as your release valve, a God-given way to restore emotional balance. Use it as often as you need.

Tears are not a sign of weakness, but a testament to our humanity. Even Jesus wept, a reminder that tears are not only acceptable but deeply meaningful. Yet I struggled to see the truth in numerous facets. My perspective clouded my ability to recognize the realities before me.

Holding Space for Others

One of the most transformative lessons I've learned is the power of holding space for others. I remember a moment with a new friend when I was overwhelmed by emotion and began to cry because what I was sharing was so personal, regarding me and my spouse. The reason I even felt like sharing was because she had such an open posture of listening; no judgment, just ears to hear with love and compassion. As I instinctively turned away to hide my tears, she gently said, "I'm not going anywhere; your tears don't scare me." That simple statement changed me. It gave me permission to cry openly and taught me that vulnerability is not something to fear.

That experience taught me that holding space is one of the most meaningful ways to love others. It's not just about listening; it's about being present, offering comfort, and giving the other person the freedom to feel and process without judgment.

There have been many times since when someone has held space for me without trying to "fix" me, and it has meant the world to me. It truly is a gift. In those moments, I've felt seen and valued for who I am, not for what they could do or how they could "fix" me. This love does not try to change a person. Instead, it focuses on being present with someone just as they are. This has deepened my relationships and taught me that sometimes the best way to show love is by offering a safe space for someone to be themselves.

In my faith, I see God doing the same for us. He holds space for our tears, knowing that they carry our deepest emotions, our pain, and our surrender. God doesn't rush us to "fix" our hearts or to stop our crying; instead, He meets us in the midst of it, offering grace and understanding. When the time is right, and I am ready, I can ask Him to help me fix whatever needs mending.

I believe the same approach applies to our relationships with others. We sit with our friends in their pain, holding space for them, and when they are ready, they can ask for our help. It's hard to do sometimes because, as women, we often feel the urge to "fix" problems immediately. But there is wisdom in stepping back and allowing others the time and space they need to grieve, heal, or process in their own way.

This doesn't mean there won't be opportunities to help or solve a problem later. It simply means prioritizing presence over solutions. The urge should be to remain present, hold space, and let them guide when they're ready for more. Then, when the time comes, you'll be there, ready to provide the support they need.

This is one of those truths I am slowly learning: God's timing is not ours. I often find myself longing for changes to happen now, but I am learning that God is patient, and that means I need to be also. He gives us the time we need to grow and transform into who He is guiding us to become. I am deeply grateful that God sees our hearts and gives us the space to stumble and learn. This also means I need to do the same for the people in my life, even when it feels like progress is impossibly slow.

There was a particular struggle I had with a close family relationship that took about three years before I finally felt at peace with it. It was one of those relationships where misunderstandings ran deep, where I often felt unseen or unsure of how to bridge the gap. Those years felt long and difficult at times, but they also served as a reminder that growth and change take time.

Looking back, I can see how God was working—not necessarily in the other person, but in me. He was teaching me patience, humility, and a deeper trust in His ability to do what I could not. I wanted resolution to come quickly, but instead, God walked me through a slow process of transformation, showing me that true peace isn't about fixing people—it's about surrendering my own heart to His work. In the end, what changed most wasn't the circumstances, but me.

I see this same waiting and believing play out in the lives of people close to me. I see God working in their hearts, slowly shaping and transforming them in ways that only He can. But if I'm honest, there are moments when it feels so slow—too slow. I find myself wrestling with impatience, longing to see the breakthroughs happen now. I want their life to be easy, their choices to align with God's will, and their healing to be complete. But God's pace is not mine, and His ways are higher than mine.

In those moments of frustration, I am reminded that God is never in a hurry. He sees the whole picture, the end from the beginning, and He knows exactly what is needed for true transformation. While I may feel like nothing is happening, God is working in ways I cannot see, planting seeds deep in their hearts that will grow in His perfect timing.

Waiting and believing alongside someone is an act of faith. It requires letting go of a desire to control the outcome and instead trusting that God's love for them is even greater than your own. Remember that when you surrender your timeline, you're surrendering it to a God filled with patience and grace for you that He can also extend to others.

What I perceive as slowness is actually part of God's mercy. He doesn't rush because He wants change to be lasting and complete. He is patient because He loves others just as He loves me. And when I think about how slow my own growth has been at times, I realize I have no room to complain.

There's a beauty in the waiting, even when it's hard. It's in these seasons of trusting and believing that I'm reminded of how deeply God cares for each of us. He doesn't leave us in our struggles, and He doesn't abandon the work He's started. Philippians 1:6 reassures me of this: "He who began a good work in you will carry it on to completion until the day of Christ Jesus." Just as God is patient with us in our own journeys, He calls us to extend that same grace and understanding to others. I've learned this doesn't mean enabling someone to stay stuck or condoning choices that hurt them. It means being present with them in their pain, praying for them, and trusting God's timing for their transformation.

When I think about God holding space for us, it reminds me that He doesn't just tolerate our tears–He values them. He sees the depth of our hearts in every tear that falls. And when I find myself in the place of waiting, whether it's for healing in my own life or in someone else's, I remember that God is not distant. He is there, holding space and inviting me to trust Him more deeply.

Jesus wept with those who mourned, reminding us that our tears are not a sign of weakness, but a beautiful, human expression of our need for His comfort. Just as God holds space for our tears, we are called to do the same for others; to be present with them in their sadness and offer a safe place for them to grieve. In these moments, we reflect God's heart and His love for us. Our tears matter. They are seen, heard, and held by Him.

A Legacy of Joy and Hope

As I reflect on my childhood and my parents, I've come to realize that no upbringing is perfect. My dad carried heavy burdens, often worrying about things beyond his control. His deep desire for his children's salvation was admirable, but the weight of that responsibility seemed to rest on his shoulders alone, stealing moments of joy. I know now that he carried those concerns with a heaviness that perhaps wasn't his to bear.

Looking back, I see the love and sincerity in his intentions, yet I also see how holding onto that kind of burden can overshadow the present. It reminds me of how God invites us to cast our cares on Him because He never meant for us to carry these things alone. My dad's story is a powerful example of what happens when we try to take on too much in our own strength, even for the noblest reasons. Learning from his example, I am determined to let go of unnecessary burdens and embrace a life centered on trust in God's sufficiency.

I don't want to live weighted down with burdens that will only hinder God's work. I want to leave behind a legacy of joy, hope, and faith for my children, a life they can look back on with gratitude. Not only that, I want them to remember a home filled with laughter, meaningful conversations, and the assurance that God was always present, even in the hard times. Life isn't about avoiding pain, but about trusting God to redeem it.

As Paul reminds us: "And we know that in all things God works for the good of those who love him, who have been called according to his purpose" (Romans 8:28).

What does that look like in everyday life? I believe it means trusting that God is weaving the threads of our lives, even the tangled and painful ones, into a greater picture of His purpose. There are times when things don't go as planned, and yet, the end result often exceeds what we initially imagined. Is that what Paul meant? I think so. It's not that everything will always be easy or pleasant, but that God, in His sovereignty, takes what is broken or disappointing and transforms it into something meaningful—something for our good and His glory.

This promise gives me hope even when I don't fully understand His plan. It reminds me to embrace life's twists and turns, trusting that every moment, both the joyful and the painful, can be used by God to fulfill His purpose in ways I may not see right away.

Hope Beyond Tears

I have hope in today and now, but there is also a hope for a brighter future, a future I don't fully comprehend, but that pulls at the heart of every child of God. This hope is both comforting and challenging. I want to be prepared as Jesus instructs, but there are times I find myself hesitating, longing for His return to wait just a little longer because there are loved ones who haven't yet accepted Him. This paradox is a reminder of God's patience, not wanting anyone to perish but for all to come to repentance (2 Peter 3:9). It motivates me to live faithfully, trusting God to work in their lives even as I cling to the hope of His promises.

Tears are a reminder of the brokenness in our world, but they also point us to the hope we have in Christ. One day, God will wipe away every tear, and there will be no more pain, sorrow, or loss.

> *"He will wipe every tear from their eyes. There will be no more death or mourning or crying or pain..."*
> *Revelation 21:4*

Until that day, we live in the balance between sorrow and hope. Our tears are not wasted; they are a part of God's redemptive story. They remind us that we are human, that we feel deeply, and that we long for the restoration only He can bring.

Conclusion: Let the Tears Flow

If you've been holding back your tears, let them flow. Allow yourself to feel the release that comes with crying out to God. Imagine Him holding you as you pour out your pain, whispering that you are loved and seen.

> *"Cast all your anxiety on Him because He cares for you."*
> *1 Peter 5:7*

Tears don't make you weak; they make you human. Trust that God is weaving your story into something beautiful, even in the midst of your struggles. A few years ago, I faced a deep trial that shook everything I believed about my life. I felt lost, overwhelmed, and utterly alone—caught in the depths of despair, truly desperate. It was a time when I questioned everything: how my life was unfolding, the foundation of my faith, and whether I could trust what I had always believed to be true.

This season of my life was marked by deep heartache and uncertainty. An intimate relationship I had trusted felt fragile, and I struggled to make sense of the pain I was experiencing. I wrestled with disappointment, doubt, and the fear that the life I had built was crumbling around me. I had always believed that if I did everything "right," things would work out, but suddenly, I was face-to-face with a reality I shrank from; I almost felt like I was going to lose it completely. The phrase "going mad" felt very real to me at the time.

Looking back, I can now see how God used that season as a stepping stone to push me out of my comfort zone. Sometimes, it takes walking through a difficult period to help you reevaluate what truly matters. These challenges, though overwhelming, are not evidence of God forgetting you. Instead, they are often where His refining work takes place. The depths of despair become the perfect ground for Him to create something new. It is where beauty is born from the ashes of broken dreams, and mourning is turned into joy.

That season changed everything for me. It redefined my priorities, my perspective, and my faith. I'll forever be grateful that I was counted worthy to go through it—not because it was easy, but because it led to transformation that only God could bring.

I began exploring personal growth by evaluating the power of my choices and the thoughts I allowed to shape my life. This journey included journaling, studying Scripture, and seeking wisdom from mentors, all of which taught me to step out of my comfort zone. It challenged me to get comfortable with uncertainty and embrace change as a part of God's refining process. This experience taught me that while tears may signal despair, they also mark the beginning of transformation when we surrender to God. He is there, behind every tear, redeeming every pain, and drawing you closer to His heart.

If you're facing a trial today, remember that God might be preparing you for growth in ways you can't yet see. See it as His favor shining on you.

Reflection Questions:

1. Reflect on a time when you cried freely in God's presence. What did you feel in that moment, and how did it shape your relationship with Him?

2. In what areas of your life are you striving for perfection instead of relying on God's grace?

3. How can you create space for someone else to process their emotions and feel seen this week?

CHAPTER 4

God Hears Your Cry

"You, Lord, hear the desire of the afflicted; you encourage them,
and you listen to their cry."
—Psalm 10:17

God Sees Our Tears and Hears Our Cries

It's easy to feel like your prayers are going no further than the ceiling. The weight of feeling unheard, unloved, and invisible is overwhelming. But let me remind you of this: God sees you. He hears you. He loves you. Not only that, but He holds you with a love so vast it is hard to comprehend. Even in your darkest moments when you wonder if anyone notices your pain, He does. He cares deeply for you.

> *"You keep track of all my sorrows. You have collected*
> *all my tears in your bottle. You have recorded each*
> *one in your book."*   *Psalm 56:8, NLT*

I was so happy to find this verse, which reinforces how much God cares about all of our sorrows, the tears we shed, and what matters most to us. Think about it: the Creator of the universe recording your sorrows and tears. He is keeping track so that He can send the help you need when the time is right.

When Truth and Lies Collide

I used to feel unloved and wondered if I mattered. Questions like, "What am I doing here?" "Do I have a purpose?" would taunt me. These questions don't come from the Father of love, but from the creator of lies. It's easy to get lost in a swirl of mixed truths and lies. Discerning between them is only possible when we anchor ourselves in God's Word. By studying His truth, we begin to understand who God really is and what He thinks of us. Through His Word, He shows us how deeply we are loved, even when life feels uncertain. Remember the verses where God keeps track.

> *"He [the devil] was a murderer from the beginning, not holding to the truth, for there is no truth in him. When he lies, he speaks his native language, for he is a liar and the father of lies."*
>
> *John 8:44*

While the father of lies may try to confuse us, the evidence of God's truth is woven into our lives. His hand can be seen in the way He guides and protects us, even when we struggle to see it clearly.

Recognizing God's Hand in Our Journey

Looking back at my life, I can see God's hand in every part of my journey. It wasn't always obvious at the moment, but over time, I've come to see how He has been smoothing out the tangles. He was orchestrating behind the scenes, guiding me, protecting me, and weaving me in ways I couldn't understand at the time.

> *"And we know that in all things God works for the good of those who love him, who have been called according to his purpose."*
>
> *Romans 8:28*

Each thread in the tapestry of my life has purpose, even those that seemed frayed or broken. Looking back strengthens my faith and helps me trust that His promises are true, even when the road ahead is unclear. I would encourage everyone to take time to reflect. It is a powerful practice.

When you take time to reflect, you start to realize how much He cares for you and what He has been doing behind the scenes to help you along the way. God is good, and He loves you very much. The significance of looking back and recognizing the role God has played in your life is a valuable practice. It builds your faith in Him. You can learn to take hold of His promises and know deeply in your heart that He hears every one of your cries and sees every tear that falls from your eyes.

Reflecting on His care for us as believers brings clarity to how He works personally in our lives. My own journey has shown me how God's hand guides us even on the most unexpected paths. I felt led to marry my husband, yet if you had asked me before, I would have said no to the idea. Attending the weekend retreat I mentioned earlier was another moment of divine direction—one I hadn't planned, yet a pivotal step in my journey. The company I am a partner with has led me to many unexpected paths and has been a catalyst for the changes I have embraced. Acceptance of people and where they are in their journey. Everyone is on a path, and we don't always know the full backstory, so we must be kind.

Being part of a community that doesn't see the world as black and white is refreshing, but also can be challenging to some long-held beliefs. I don't feel like it is leading me on the wrong path, but it has definitely made me question some things. I just want you to know that it is good to be challenged in what you believe or think you believe. I feel it can make you a stronger believer in Christ. His foundation is solid and sure, and that is where you will find complete rest and peace.

Even writing this book has been a process of discovering how God weaves together the pieces of our lives. It all came together in bits and fragments—threads that, at first, seemed disconnected. Yet, looking back, I can see how God was guiding me toward the right people, the right moments, and the right opportunities to bring this dream to life. So many threads, woven together into a beautiful tapestry that only God could create.

The direction my life has taken has been by the hand of God. I must believe this; otherwise, the foundation I've been standing on wouldn't be solid. If I couldn't trust that God has been leading me all along, I would struggle to know anything for certain.

Change often requires stepping away from the familiar. I know this well. I don't know why I felt led to join the Holdeman Mennonite church group, only that I must trust God had a hand in it. Their beliefs were similar to those I grew up with in some ways, yet dramatically different in others. In one sense, I felt comfortable because of those shared values, but in another, it was a challenge to embrace a new way of life. The similarities were that women in this community wore only dresses, avoided makeup, and most stayed home rather than working outside the home. The men were farmers or carpenters—never involved in political jobs. Higher education, particularly attending college away from home, was strongly discouraged. Online education, however, was seen as an acceptable alternative, a safer way to gain knowledge while remaining within the home environment.

One noticeable difference between my upbringing and the new group I had joined was the absence of musical instruments. My father played the piano, as did some of my siblings. Music had always been a part of my home: my brother loved to play the guitar, and another brother played the drums, and we would sing together. He even had a band for a while. But in this new community, playing instruments was considered wrong. Listening to music with instruments was discouraged. However, a cappella singing was embraced and held in high regard. Their voices blended in perfect harmony, creating a depth of worship that was undeniably moving. At times, I found myself appreciating the simplicity of unaccompanied singing, realizing how it allowed the words and melodies to stand on their own without distraction.

I don't know that I thought much about missing my dad's playing and singing with my brother's band, because in many ways, I was focused on embracing everything this new community taught. I wanted to fit in, to adopt their ways as my own. Perhaps, in that effort, I pushed aside certain parts of my past, even the ones that had once brought me joy. Or maybe it was simply easier not to dwell on what I had left behind.

But the past has a way of resurfacing when you take the time to process life and all that you've been through. Memories, emotions, and unanswered questions come back in ways you don't always expect. And yet, I don't know that I need to find a place for all of them. Some things are meant to be remembered, while others are best released.

I tend to believe that isn't where God wants my focus to be. Instead, I need to dwell on the things I can change—the choices in front of me, the direction I am being led. I need to be clear on what those things look like and then leave the rest in His care.

Adopting this new way of life wasn't easy. Some changes came naturally, while others took time and effort to fully accept. I don't think many people truly appreciate what it means to leave behind familiarity and step into an entirely new way of life. It's easy to become complacent, and the idea of change can feel overwhelming. But I have learned that change—especially the kind that draws us closer to God—can be deeply transformative.

> *"Trust in the Lord with all your heart and lean not on your own understanding; in all your ways submit to him, and he will make your paths straight."*
> *Proverbs 3:5–6*

I often reflect on the impact of this small group of believers, the Holdeman Mennonites, in the grander context of the world. They accepted me into their church, but it had to be on their terms. Joining meant leaving behind the traditions and practices I had known. In my upbringing, solid-colored dresses were the norm, while printed fabrics were never part of my everyday life. Our home was simple, but stepping into this new community made me realize just how plain our surroundings truly were in comparison.

Does Jesus require all the things that were required of me? Did He ask me to do all those things, or were they just a reflection of imperfect people trying to live right to the best of their knowledge? These questions have shaped my faith journey, reminding me that God is with me through every transition. I am grateful that I can trust the hands of God guiding me. Trust that He's weaving even the challenging parts into a story of redemption and growth.

I know God was with me then, and He is still with me now. It is my anchor.

While my story reflects God's personal guidance, it also makes me ponder His greater plan for the countless lives He watches over. Like being in an airplane and flying over a city and knowing there are countless people down there and God knows every single one of them. It's almost hard to comprehend the significance of this. God knows, God sees, and God cares.

God's Plan for the Many

The billions of people who live in this world—where are they in God's plan? It's not a question I expect an answer to. It's a question I often ponder. God knows, and He hears everyone crying out to Him, even those who don't know Him personally.

> *"For I know the plans I have for you," declares the Lord, "plans to prosper you and not to harm you, plans to give you hope and a future." Jeremiah 29:11*

I know that maybe someday I will understand why I was led here, but I also want to be okay even if I don't understand. God has His ways, and we are to follow and be obedient to Him. His plans are not always how we plan them to be. Trusting that He has good intentions for us and wants to bless us beyond what we imagine can be difficult, but it is necessary. I know people might say, "I don't know if I can trust God." But if you can't trust God, whom are you trusting? Yourself? How is that working for you?

The reality is, there isn't much you can control beyond what you allow into your life. So many things lie beyond our control, but one thing you always have influence over is your choices and actions. Trusting God doesn't mean everything will be easy or that you'll understand everything in the moment. It means believing that He sees the bigger picture and is weaving it all for your good.

Hard times come to everyone; they're not a sign that God doesn't care. We live in a world that's broken by sin, corrupted and filled with evil, where hardship exists as a natural consequence. Believing in God doesn't exempt us from pain, but it does give us the assurance that we're not alone in it. God promises to walk with us through the most challenging parts of life, offering His strength, comfort, and guidance when we need it most. The question is: Will you trust Him to carry you through, or will you rely on yourself and the things you cannot control?

The Purpose in Challenges

Life is filled with challenges that can feel overwhelming. I've often wondered why we face so much pain and discord. Why does life have to be this way? The answer lies in the fact that our reality is that we live in a fallen world. But even in this brokenness, God's presence remains. Generational cycles of discord and pain can weigh heavily on us, but God offers freedom. He doesn't want us to live burdened by the chains of our past. Instead, He calls us to seek peace, rest, and a deeper understanding of His love.

Change is hard and often uncomfortable, but it is worth it. It takes courage, persistence, and faith to step into a new way of living. Each step forward adds a new, vibrant thread to the story God is weaving in our lives. Challenges, while difficult, refine us and draw us closer to Him. They are threads of a darker hue that contrast beautifully with the brighter moments, making the tapestry of our lives richer and more meaningful. He hears every cry and collects every tear. He keeps track.

If we can accept that we will have challenges, it will help us not to resist the difficult things so much. It doesn't mean it will be easy just because you accept it. It means that it will be easier because you believe that God has your back and is interested in every part of your life. He understands all the things we go through as humans. When you start paying attention to the things that happen, and if you are a believer, you will see His hands throughout your journey.

This has been my experience.

> *"Consider it pure joy, my brothers and sisters, when-*
> *ever you face trials of many kinds, because you know*
> *that the testing of your faith produces perseverance."*
> *James 1:2–3*

The challenges we face often reveal God's care in unexpected ways. This was especially true during my father's illness, a time of deep hardship but also profound reminders of God's presence.

A Father's Journey

I know when Dad was sick, we all prayed that he would be healed and get better. As I look back at that time, it was quite hard. I know God was with us and heard us. He knew we wanted Dad to get better and have a good life. Dad had gotten sick with malaria after visiting my sister and her family in Ghana. He had chosen not to take the prescribed medicine, so when he came home and ended up in the hospital, it was serious. He almost died, but by some miracle, he was helped by a nurse and doctor who happened to be in the hospital and recognized Dad's symptoms. Was it a mere coincidence, or just another one of God's ways of caring for His children? Even when we choose one way, God continues to love and care for us. It may have been the prayers we had prayed for Dad that made the difference.

I believe every prayer is answered, just not exactly as we think it is supposed to be. But, by having his symptoms understood, they could give him the right treatment, and that made all the difference for Dad to improve quickly.

Seven months later, Dad had a seizure, so he ended up in the hospital again. He was about ready to be released when he started being lethargic and wasn't responding well. He had a brain bleed caused by one of the medications he was given. It was necessary for his treatment, but was supposed to be monitored because one of the side effects was brain bleeds. Dad had to be airlifted to Nashville, where they performed emergency surgery to remove part of his skull to relieve pressure on his brain.

It was many months of slow recovery. Through it all, Dad improved and was doing quite well, but it took a lot of work. He would walk for hours as soon as he was able to get around again. He steadily got better in every way and could attend to his own needs. As soon as he was able, he even started going out with the boys to ride around. I know he was so anxious to get back to work and do what he used to do, but it wasn't meant to be.

Months later, he got sick with pneumonia. After so much improvement, this was another setback. Dad getting to hold his grandchildren after his sickness and ordeals were special moments, memories we hold close. These tender moments are the golden threads in the tapestry of our lives, reminders of His unending care.

> *"Praise be to the God and Father of our Lord Jesus Christ, the Father of compassion and the God of all comfort, who comforts us in all our troubles..."*
> *2 Corinthians 1:3–4*

Even in the uncertainty of my father's illness, I learned to trust that God was present. That trust has continued to sustain me through other moments when His plans weren't immediately clear. I had nothing else to hold on to but God. He has been the only constant in my life, and I love the beauty of it all.

The beautiful tapestry being unveiled with every thread He is weaving–the threads of gold, dark threads of pain, and the vibrant colorful threads of friendship and support we receive from others. We are all connected, and God is in the center of it all. I hold on to

His love, and believing that He heard every one of my cries was a foundational truth I could depend on.

Trusting God's Plan

In June, we all traveled to Texas for a family wedding. That's when Dad's health took another turn. Despite all this, there were moments of God's love shining through. I remember my youngest daughter hugging my dad on a porch that day after the wedding. That moment felt sacred, a reminder that God's love surrounds us even in the hardest times. Later that day, he was airlifted again, and we faced hard decisions. Was this God's plan? Despite our pain and uncertainty, we trusted His hand through it all.

Not every prayer is answered in the way we hope. You've read this far in my story and now know some of the challenges I faced growing up. I want to make it clear that over the years, Dad did change. He came to see the truth of what Jesus had to offer, and I am so thankful that he was able to let go of striving for perfect performance and embrace the gift of redemption.

When Dad passed away, it was hard not to question if we had done enough or made the right decisions. Should we have tried harder to keep him going, knowing it might have meant him living the rest of his days bedridden? If Dad could have shared his thoughts with us, we know he would have said that it would have been the worst outcome for him. These questions lingered, but I am learning to trust that God's plans are beyond my understanding. His timing and purpose often remain a mystery, yet I've come to find peace in knowing that His love never falters. Even when we don't understand, He is weaving something beautiful out of our tears and prayers.

> *"For my thoughts are not your thoughts, neither are your ways my ways," declares the Lord. "As the heav-*

*ens are higher than the earth, so are my ways higher
than your ways and my thoughts than your thoughts."*
Isaiah 55:8–9

Even now, I am learning to carry the lessons from those moments into my daily life. Trusting God's plan wasn't just about navigating the pain of losing Dad; it's about surrendering my own fears and uncertainties today.

I wrestle with limiting beliefs that hold me back. What if I'm not enough? What if I fail? These doubts are barriers to the life God wants for me. Trusting Him means stepping out of my comfort zone, even when it feels safer to stay where I am. Vulnerability is scary, but it is also where growth begins. Every time I surrender a fear or doubt to God, I add a thread of trust and faith to His design.

God's Perfect Weaving

As I reflect on all these experiences, I see now that life is a tapestry. You have one too, one that God is weaving. Some threads are dark and painful, while others are golden and full of joy. Yet, each thread has its place in the masterpiece God is creating. Even in the moments when we can't see the full picture, we can trust that His design is perfect.

Faith doesn't mean understanding everything. It means trusting God's goodness, even when His ways don't make sense. As Lysa TerKeurst, from Proverbs 31 Ministries, writes in her devotional, *If You're Walking a Road That's Still Really Hard,* "Faith in God means being assured of His goodness even when what He allows doesn't feel good, seem good, or look good right now."[3] We may not have

---

3   TerKeurst, Lysa. "If You're Walking a Road That's Still Really Hard." *Proverbs 31 Ministries,* 9 Sept. 2024, https://proverbs31.org/read/devotions/full-post/2024/09/09/if-youre-walking-a-road-thats-still-really-hard.

all the answers, but we can rest in the assurance that God hears our cries and loves us deeply. The answers often aren't what we expect, but that's where trust comes in, trusting that God is weaving our past, present, and future into something beautiful.

> "He has made everything beautiful in its time. He has also set eternity in the human heart; yet no one can fathom what God has done from beginning to end."
> Ecclesiastes 3:11

God doesn't promise us a life without pain, but He does promise to be with us through it all. He sees every tear, hears every cry, and works all things together for good in ways we may never understand on this side of eternity.

So, I leave you with this: trust the Master Weaver. Know that He is at work, creating something beautiful out of your story. Even when the road is hard, even when prayers feel unanswered, He is weaving His love and grace into every moment. And one day, we will see the fullness of His plan and marvel at the beauty He has created in our lives.

Reflection Questions:

1. Where have you seen God's hand working in your life, even if it wasn't obvious at first?
2. How do you handle moments when God's plans don't align with your expectations?
3. What steps can you take to trust God more deeply with the unanswered prayers and challenges in your life?

PART 2

Eyes Are Opened: Learning to Let God of the Stories and Patterns of My Past

"Do not be conformed to this world, but be transformed by the renewal of your mind, that by testing you may discern what is the will of God, what is good and acceptable and perfect."

Romans 12:2, ESV

CHAPTER 5

Awareness: A Gift

"Awareness is the greatest agent for change."[4]
—Eckhart Tolle

The Power of Self-Awareness

Awareness—such an important concept—is often overlooked in our community. Many people live their lives guided by unexamined thoughts and emotions, unaware of the control they actually have. For me, realizing this truth was transformative. It opened my eyes to the fact that I didn't have to sit passively and let life happen to me. I discovered that God has woven His purpose into our ability to respond thoughtfully and intentionally to life's challenges.

As Proverbs 4:23 reminds us, "Above all else, guard your heart, for everything you do flows from it."

This Scripture emphasizes the importance of being mindful of our thoughts and emotions, as they shape our actions and decisions. God's Word teaches that we are responsible for our thoughts and what we allow into our lives, aligning perfectly with the concept of awareness.

Life happens, and the truth is, you are in control of your reaction.

---

4   Tolle, Eckhart. *A New Earth: Awakening to Your Life's Purpose*. Penguin Group, 2005.

But you have to be aware of this fact if you want to have a life that is meaningful and fulfilling. People who live without self-awareness are missing a vital part of living a wonderful life. Without self-awareness, life becomes reactive rather than intentional. Decisions are made based on habit, external pressure, or fleeting emotions rather than a deep understanding of who we are and what truly matters. Instead of steering their lives with purpose, they are carried along by circumstances, unaware of the patterns and choices that shape their experiences.

Self-awareness allows us to recognize our thoughts, emotions, and behaviors, giving us the power to make better choices. Without it, we may find ourselves repeating the same mistakes, engaging in relationships that drain us, or pursuing goals that don't truly align with who we are. People who lack self-awareness often struggle with unresolved emotions, leading to misunderstandings, frustration, or even conflict in their relationships.

Practical Steps to Growth

Self-awareness is an awareness of one's own personality and individuality. It plays a critical role in daily life, influencing how we interact with others, respond to challenges, and make decisions. For example, when my child spills something, if I am self-aware, I can recognize whether my reaction is calm or out of frustration. This awareness helps me choose a more constructive response. By staying curious about our reactions and emotions, we gain valuable insights into ourselves, leading to more thoughtful actions and better relationships. Stay curious about your reaction and emotions around different situations and people. You can learn a lot about yourself, and it really does make a difference in how you behave and what you say. What you are thinking is another area that, when you are aware, you stay curious about your thoughts.

Steps to growth stem from being aware. For instance, you might begin by noticing patterns in your reactions, such as feeling frustrated in specific situations. Questions like "Why do I feel this way?" or "What past experience does this remind me of?" can lead to valuable insights and emotional healing. Growth also involves actions like practicing mindfulness, seeking counsel, and praying for God's wisdom. Awareness, guided by faith, becomes a foundation for transformation. By aligning our thoughts with God's purpose, as we invite Him into our journey,

Psalm 139:23–24 reminds us: "Search me, God, and know my heart; test me and know my anxious thoughts. See if there is any offensive way in me, and lead me in the way everlasting." For instance, when you recognize a recurring pattern or trigger, you can reflect deeply: "Why did I react this way?" or "How can I approach this differently next time?" It's not merely about noticing, but actively engaging with your emotions and responses.

Psalm 139:23–24 illustrates how inviting God's perspective into our self-awareness fosters deeper growth. By doing this, we align our actions with His purpose and embrace His grace in our personal transformation. Awareness becomes a foundation for meaningful change in every aspect of life. If your desire is to grow, it will help you do so, and you will become a better person. I believe Jesus is the One who completes us, but I also believe that He works through different avenues in our lives to accomplish His purpose.

I like noticing the way we do things and how growth comes from learning and doing life differently. It is important to acknowledge our growth and to see how far we have come. The glory needs to go to God, because it is only by His grace that we are able to be vibrant and thriving Christians.

As has been the case for so many things in my life, I didn't know what awareness meant or how it all worked. Furthermore, I didn't have the vocabulary for my emotions. Yes, I knew being sad and mad, feeling shame and guilt. I didn't have the words for feeling frustration, uncertainty, nervousness, and unworthiness, all the emotions that tell different stories about what is going on inside. Trying to express emotions wasn't in my family's vocabulary. I don't know why we didn't talk about our feelings; it may have stemmed from the fact that dwelling on ourselves was discouraged, all in the name of living a humble life.

I want to explain what I mean by struggling to find the right words to express my feelings. We were raised to live a simple life, without any fuss about things, and we were taught to use straightforward language. This simple lifestyle consisted of waking up, going to work or school depending on our age, coming home, and going to bed. There wasn't much excitement. I didn't think it was a bad way to live.

My greatest regret about how we lived is that joy wasn't abundant. And in a Christian's experience, joy should abound. It is right and good to learn how to express yourself. When you take time to name your emotions, it is beneficial to yourself and others. I have found it helps me when I can pause and name my emotions or even acknowledge whatever I am feeling. When you name it or acknowledge it, it almost lessens the intensity of whatever is going on.

Maybe giving it room makes it not seem like a bad thing. In my mind, if I felt anything other than happy, I was missing something. Now, I know that emotions are just indicators, and they don't define you or make you bad. Just like when the engine light is on in your car, you can ignore it, but eventually something will happen and you will have to do something about it. This is just like your emotions; you can ignore them for only so long. But there will come a point in time when you will erupt, and you will be left floundering in the chaos of it all.

As Galatians 5:22–23 states, "But the fruit of the Spirit is love, joy, peace, forbearance, kindness, goodness, faithfulness, gentleness and self-control." This gentle and vibrant sense of joy and peace comes not from external circumstances, but from living in alignment with the Spirit and knowing whose you are. It doesn't mean you are giddy and giggly all the time, but it does create a gentle and vibrant sense of peace which results in joy because of whose you are.

The Connection Between Simplicity and Awareness

Simple living is a lost art. The practice of simplicity fosters awareness and connects us more deeply to God's presence. By stepping away from the distractions of constant busyness and material pursuits, we create space to notice the beauty of creation, the flow of our emotions, and the quiet guidance of the Holy Spirit in our lives. Simple living allows us to align with God's purpose, nurturing a life of intention and gratitude. This mindful approach allows us to be more intentional in our thoughts, actions, and relationships, ultimately leading to a more grounded and fulfilled life.

We can become so focused on doing and having that simple living seems less interesting. An example of simple living is having a farm where you grow your own food and raise animals for whatever needs you have. Having everything fresh is a lot of work, but it is more about being connected to nature and to the source, which is now a rarity. I don't really know how to get on that track; it's not that I think I have to live this kind of lifestyle, but there is something appealing about it.

Life is supposed to be simple, but it's not easy. Life moves fast—too fast. It can feel like we're all passengers on a train that never stops, hurtling forward at full speed without a clear destination. We rush from task to task, meeting to meeting, screen to screen, trying to keep up with the pace the world sets for us. But at the end of the day, what do we actually have to show for all that motion? Have we arrived anywhere that truly matters? It isn't about more stuff or more knowledge. We are the most informed generation of our time, but we are also some of the unhappiest people.

Some want to blame technology, social media, and other things, but isn't that giving your power away? I love technology. I love the convenience, the tools, the possibilities. Not only that, but I do believe we can get sucked into unhealthy practices, but again what are you choosing? It is up to you what you allow to take over in your life.

But do I really crave a simple life? The honest answer? Yes and no.

Some days, I dream of stepping off the train entirely—of escaping to a quiet place where fresh air fills my lungs and the mountains remind me to breathe deeply, a place where life slows down and the frantic noise of the world fades into the background. But is that truly the solution? Is it realistic to believe a simple life is only found somewhere far away?

What if simplicity isn't about geography, but about awareness? What if living well isn't about running away, but about being present wherever you are?

Instead of chasing after an ideal version of life, I want to use the resources God has given me to live well aware—aware of what truly matters, aware of what I'm saying yes to, and aware of when to step back from the noise. Maybe I don't need to jump off the train entirely to escape, but by learning how to be present, lessen stress, and hold onto peace no matter how fast life moves around me. I am simplifying my life with choices that align with who I want to be.

The Weight of Stress and the Power of Awareness

Stress can make life hard, regardless of how simple you are living. That is what I feel took my dad. He didn't know how to handle stress and things that were out of his control. I want to say this with lots of love, because the truth is, Dad was living his life to the best of his knowledge he had at the time.

That's why I want to live differently—not by avoiding life's complexities, but by learning how to walk through them with awareness. Lately, I've been reading about the toll stress takes on our bodies and health; it's serious. Stress can kill you.

We have become addicted to stress. I see it everywhere—people constantly rushing, constantly worried, constantly weighed down. We live in a world that is stressed out by everything—work, finances, relationships, expectations, and the constant pull of technology. It's easy to get caught in that never-ending cycle.

But I don't want to live that way.

We may never live in a completely stress-free environment, but I do believe we can live with a lot less stress than we do right now. It starts with awareness.

I didn't always understand the power of awareness. But looking back, I can see how God was gently weaving change into my life long before I recognized it. His grace was there, nudging me, teaching me, showing me a different way to live. A way that isn't ruled by stress, but by peace.

And maybe that's the answer—not escaping stress altogether, but learning how to live well in the midst of it.

I grew up, eventually got married, and I learned to say "I love you" to my husband. I don't know why it was so hard, but those weren't words I had heard often. It may seem like a simple thing, but saying "I love you" is very important. I did love him as much as I understood those terms. I didn't hear those words as I was growing up.

Of course, I knew my parents cared about me. After getting married, quite a few years passed before my parents would audibly say they loved us. It was a little awkward at first, but gradually, I became more comfortable saying it back, and I am happy to say it isn't hard to say those words now.

It is a comfort to me that God creates change, but it takes time to bring good changes into your life so that it can be different. In these changes, God is behind the scenes and always working on the details. Untangling and then weaving in beauty despite the frayed or broken threads of our lives.

Even though you might at times feel alone, you really are loved and cared for. Remember this: God loves you unconditionally, and He knows all the intricate details about your life. He has a purpose for you that only you can fulfill. Only you.

When Self-Reflection Was Discouraged: Rediscovering God's Intent for Awareness

Growing up, life had its challenges, and trying to understand what and how my parents believed wasn't always easy. Dad's parents taught their children that dwelling on themselves was a form of pride. Being mindful of our appearance wasn't encouraged. I see how they wanted to be neat and orderly, but definitely nothing too pretty or colorful. I know they couldn't help some of that because it is what they were taught. As I look at creation, I have to wonder how we can deny that color was part of God's plan. If being plain was so important, why did He make the world so vibrant? We are naturally drawn to colors, textures, and designs—things that make us unique. If colors were truly wrong, wouldn't God have created the earth in only a few shades? Did He really intend for us to live as bland, muted versions of ourselves? I suppose I can try to see it from their perspective, but I'm not sure if I fully understand.

The belief that was passed down to us is that we are created beings meant to be humble and plain. This idea is tied back to Lucifer—how he was beautiful, became proud, and sought to be equal with God. The thinking was that if you remained as plain as possible, you could avoid the temptation of pride. It's somewhat sad, but I understand that they were truly doing their best based on their beliefs. I don't mean to suggest that I know better than they did; everything I'm sharing is simply my perspective. If you asked someone else, you might hear a different story.

Self-reflection, self-awareness—essentially anything that involves "self"—was not to be considered. "Self" leads to pride. Self-care was deemed out of the question, not even seen as a beneficial or godly practice. There is still some controversy about this practice, especially in conservative circles where self-care is often seen as selfish rather than a means of honoring God with our bodies and minds. The self-care I want you to practice is one where you spend time with God, take good care of your health, and go outside to get fresh air and release tension.

Pride was considered a sin to be constantly monitored. This meant examining daily choices and actions, such as how we dressed, spoke, and maintained our homes, to ensure they didn't reflect arrogance or self-importance. Every decision was filtered through a lens of humility, emphasizing staying centered and steering clear of anything that might create a sense of superiority.

Because pride is what led to Lucifer's fall from heaven, it was regarded with the utmost seriousness in my upbringing. This belief deeply influenced our daily lives, shaping practices and behaviors to avoid anything perceived as prideful. Everything was measured against the standard of humility, ensuring we didn't fall into the same sin.

The Bible does speak against pride, and it was a big thing that came into play with what happened. There is the evil pride, the one that separates you from God, where you place yourself above His wisdom and guidance. This kind of pride manifests in arrogance, refusal to listen, and insistence on having your way. In contrast, there is a healthy pride that comes from taking care of the gifts God has entrusted to you, such as maintaining your home, working diligently, or stewarding relationships well. This healthy pride reflects gratitude and responsibility, acknowledging that all good things come from Him.

To help you understand their mindset and way of life, it was clear that they valued simplicity and humility above all else. This often meant avoiding anything that might appear extravagant or self-indulgent. Their choices in clothing, home decor, and even gardening reflected a desire to stay plain and unassuming, which they believed aligned with God's call for humility.

Plainness and Humility: A Misguided Pursuit?

Plainness was considered the opposite of being haughty or lifted up. It was a deliberate choice to avoid anything that might reflect pride or self-importance. Rarely did you see flowers in gardens planted for the sake of beauty alone; instead, they were chosen for practical purposes, such as repelling insects. The idea was simple: if something appeared too beautiful, it could lead to excessive pride, and that would be your downfall.

This mindset extended to all areas of life—plain clothes, plain houses, and muted colors. Bright colors, pastels, or anything that might draw attention were frowned upon. The goal was to see oneself as "the lowest of the low," which was equated with humility. While this way of life was rooted in sincere faith and a desire to honor God, it also unintentionally suppressed expressions of individuality and joy, qualities I now see as essential to God's purpose for us.

Looking back, I can understand where this thinking came from. My parents and their community genuinely believed that humility required avoiding anything that could be seen as showy or extravagant. Their efforts were well-intentioned, but they missed an important truth: God created beauty and color as part of His magnificent design. To reject these gifts entirely is to overlook the joy and creativity He has woven into His creation.

I know education can bring its own set of evils, but a little education and exposure to other ways of living and thinking can help you to grow and become more grounded in the true foundation. If you live your life merely following what you were taught without taking the time to understand the reasons behind it, you may be missing something vital to your personal growth journey. Awareness needs to be part of this growth. You grow stronger by having challenges in your life.

A little challenge to your beliefs shouldn't shake you—it should make you want to know and be anchored in the truth. Blind faith in others and the community may feel easy because it doesn't require you to wrestle with hard questions or examine what you truly believe. It allows you to simply accept what you are told without questioning its foundation. But real faith is strengthened through seeking, learning, and growing—becoming steadfast and solid.

Without a strong foundation, you are like a tree sheltered from strong winds, preventing its roots from growing deep. When that protection is removed, the tree may topple over. To ensure stability, it's important to know the truth and be firmly rooted in a solid foundation. The ultimate source of that foundation is God through Jesus Christ.

Living Intentionally Through Awareness

You may wonder how to bring more awareness into your life. This journey begins with humility and prayer, as Psalm 139:23–24 beautifully illustrates: "Search me, God, and know my heart; test me and know my anxious thoughts. See if there is any offensive way in me, and lead me in the way everlasting."

Awareness means being mindful of your thoughts, emotions, and surroundings. For example, imagine a conversation where someone makes a dismissive comment. Instead of reacting defensively, awareness enables you to pause and reflect: "Why did that comment affect me? Is there something deeper being triggered?" This reflective practice invites God's perspective into our reactions, leading to deeper understanding and transformation. This process not only helps you respond thoughtfully but also leads to greater understanding of yourself and the dynamics at play. I believe everyone should ask questions about their life's path and consider how they can improve, be better, and show up more authentically.

When you live in a state of awareness, you are apt to make intentional choices, improve relationships, and benefit your overall well-being. Awareness is key to personal growth and emotional regulation. Asking questions does not mean questioning your faith. Faith withstands the questioning of your foundational beliefs. Do you know what your foundational beliefs are? What are they set on? Shifting sand or solid rock? The solid rock is Jesus, who died for you. If you believe this, you are rooted in the truth.

Have faith in Jesus and the work He did on the cross so that you can be free. As John 8:36 says, "So if the Son sets you free, you will be free indeed." This freedom is not just from sin, but from the burdens of trying to prove our worth or striving to meet the expectations of others. Similarly, Romans 6:22 highlights this transformation: "But now that you have been set free from sin and have become slaves of God, the benefit you reap leads to holiness, and the result is eternal life." These verses emphasize the profound spiritual and personal liberation that comes through Christ. We are free from working to be good enough, to be everything for everyone, free to be who God made us to be, and free to say thank you, Jesus, for loving me enough to die. We are free to accept that He covered all the sins in our lives. Jesus brings freedom.

Embrace all of this with faith, as faith in God is essential for achieving success in life. This isn't just about financial success, though. He can bless that aspect of your life as well. Rather, I mean success in terms of living a joyful and peace-filled life, grounded in the assurance of Jesus' love.

Faith and Awareness Working Together

Be aware of your limited knowledge and recognize where you may need God's help. This humility is foundational in aligning your life with His will. While God's Word holds the ultimate answers, it's important to seek His guidance without bias or preconceived notions. Growing up, I observed how interpretations of Scripture were often shaped by traditions rather than God's intent.

True awareness involves approaching His Word with a seeking heart, asking for His wisdom, and committing to live out His purpose faithfully. How easy it is to do depends on how much you care about fulfilling God's will. God's power isn't limited by the things you do or believe. If you are seeking, searching, longing to be a follower of Jesus, God will make a way for you.

Along with awareness, my emotional intelligence was limited. In my experiences as a child and youth, one word covered all the things which aren't always helpful: mad. It could mean angry, frustrated, jealous, hatred, uncertain, uncomfortable, nervous, and maybe some other emotions. Sad could mean fearful, scared, uncertain, mad, the need to hide, tearful, and alone. Understanding your emotions is so important to being a healthy individual navigating this world.

Being able to articulate what you are feeling is very beneficial. I don't think many realize the importance of this skill. If you don't have emotional intelligence, it's not too late; you can still gain knowledge in these necessary skills.

If you want to be a healthy, emotionally intelligent, grounded, and aware person, the skills below are ones you need to learn. When I learned some of these concepts, I do believe it made me become a better person. In this practice, you are not allowed to judge your thoughts or emotions. You pay attention to them and find ways to deal with whatever is going on. It helps you become a more open person with less judgment on yourself, which in turn helps you not have so much judgment towards other people.

When you hold yourself to a set of standards and ideals, it's likely that you impose similar expectations on others. While this may not be your intention, I've found myself doing just that in my interactions with people. I struggled to have grace for others because I lacked grace for myself. It's important to release judgment, especially if it has been a recurring theme in your life. Let go of judging your thoughts and emotions. Instead, take time to reflect on them. Ask God for guidance in identifying what needs to change and how you can go about making those changes.

Emotional Awareness for Personal Growth

Being aware of and noticing your emotions can make you a better person. When something upsets you and brings strong feelings in your body, take time to notice it and ask questions. Why do I feel this way? When have I felt this way before? Where am I feeling it? Different situations bring different emotions, and they trigger your body. Your body will tell you something is up even before you feel the emotions. Pay attention to what your body is telling you.

The ability to regulate your emotions will bring more peace into your life. Awareness is one step, and emotional regulation is another. Awareness means recognizing that you're feeling something—whether it's frustration, anxiety, joy, or sadness—without immediately reacting to it. It's that moment of noticing, "Oh, I'm feeling really tense right now." Instead of pushing emotions aside or letting them take control, awareness allows you to pause and acknowledge what's happening inside you.

Emotional regulation takes it a step further—it's naming your emotions without judgment and deciding how to respond. It doesn't mean ignoring or suppressing feelings, but rather managing them in a way that aligns with your well-being and values. For example, if you feel overwhelmed, regulation might look like taking deep breaths, stepping away for a moment, or choosing to respond calmly instead of snapping in frustration When you develop both of these skills, you become a happier, more relaxed person—someone others naturally want to be around.

Using these skills when dealing with my children has helped me tremendously. I don't do it perfectly by any means, but I work on becoming better every day. Some days, I feel like I'm moving backward, but I've learned to give myself grace. Mistakes will happen, and that's okay—I won't get it right all the time, but that doesn't mean I'm failing.

Understanding that your emotions are telling you something can be life-changing. When you take time to pause and reflect, you start uncovering answers. This doesn't mean you are constantly overanalyzing your thoughts and feelings. Instead, it becomes a quiet awareness playing in the background of your mind, shaping how you respond to life. It's a beautiful, God-given ability—one that, when tuned into, can help you live more intentionally and walk in the purpose He has for you.

I have been so grateful for being introduced to this concept of awareness. Life is already hard—we don't need to make it harder by living without understanding. Awareness brings clarity, helps you stay in tune with your surroundings, and allows you to notice the things that truly matter. When you are in tune, you will not only see more, but you will also be able to be more and do more in alignment with the life God has called you to.

For thirty-nine years, I lived without the knowledge of awareness and understanding my emotions. Of course, when you are a young child, that isn't entirely your fault (but sometimes, I think children have an innate ability to express themselves authentically). Children will express themselves freely *unless* they are shut down. If and when they are shut down, they learn to hide their feelings and thoughts, which only builds up because there isn't a safe space for them to release. Children can grow up with the idea that feelings are bad and meant to be hidden. They are taught not to speak their mind in case they share something bad. Maybe that isn't how childhood was for you, but it was that way for me.

So many of these things were wrong interpretations of the things that I heard. My perspective wasn't always on track. Does this mean I was wrong? Perhaps it indicates I had learned to view things differently than my parents intended.

Our surroundings and what we hear (or think we hear) influence everything we think and do. There is always a reason why we do what we do and why we think a certain way. This isn't about being right or wrong. I want you to understand that even with the best training, you can still make mistakes.

I used to believe that I had to behave in a certain way to be right with God. However, I now realize how deeply He loves me. He sent His Son, who willingly chose to die for me, so that I wouldn't have to prove my worth. My worth was already established and recognized, and I was deemed worthy of redemption.

What does awareness have to do with Jesus dying on the cross? I think it has to do with everything. How aware are you of what that must have cost Jesus? How aware are you of what God actually did by sending Jesus? How aware are you of what you feel and how that affects the people around you? These are questions you may want to take time to think about and answer honestly from deep within your heart.

God has given you the gift of Jesus. He has also given you the gifts of your emotions, and He has a way for you to learn and grow to live well with these complexities of your being.

Reflection Questions:

1. What patterns in your emotions or reactions do you notice, and how might these patterns reveal areas for growth?

2. How does the idea of aligning your awareness with God's purpose change the way you approach daily decisions?

3. In what ways can you practice healthy pride and gratitude for the gifts God has entrusted to you while remaining humble?

CHAPTER 6

Unburden Your Load

"Life is really simple, but we insist on making it complicated"[5]
—Confucius

What Does It Mean to Be Unburdened?

Imagine walking through a crowded airport, lugging an overstuffed suitcase. It's heavy, awkward, and every step feels like a chore. A friend approaches and says, "Let me take that for you." As you reluctantly hand it over, the weight vanishes, and relief washes over you. That's what it means to be unburdened: to allow someone else to carry what you no longer can hold.

God knows the weight of everything we carry. I've often felt crushed under the weight of expectations, mostly ones I placed on myself. Over time, I've learned to release those burdens to Him. Yet I've also found myself picking them up again, requiring me to pray and surrender them anew. Even that tendency used to feel burdensome, but I've come to see it as part of the process of trusting God.

What would it look like to lay your burdens down? Would you feel lighter, freer, or maybe even a little lost? Sometimes, the weight we carry becomes so much a part of us that letting it go feels

---

5 Direct citation is not available. Concepts aligned with information found by Confucius.

strange, even frightening. It's as if the burden itself has defined us for so long that its absence creates uncertainty.

Consider what you're carrying today. Are you weighed down by expectations, your own or those placed on you by others? Do you feel crushed by guilt for not measuring up? For not being enough? These burdens can feel overwhelming, almost inescapable.

In the midst of our striving, there is hope: "Come to me, all you who are weary and burdened, and I will give you rest" (Matthew 11:28). God doesn't just promise relief, He promises rest—a deep soul-rest that frees us from striving and invites us to trust. Yet so often, we resist. We hold onto our burdens because they feel familiar, even when heavy and painful.

I've been there. For years, I carried burdens that weren't mine to bear. I believed they were my responsibility, but all they did was weigh me down and keep me from the joy God wanted for me. It's like stagnant water. Without the movement of fresh, clean water, it grows murky and lifeless.

The burdens I carried weren't from God; they were the expectations placed on me by others, rules and standards that had nothing to do with what He truly requires of me. I don't believe God is overly concerned with whether the print on my dress has flowers that are too large, how many square feet my house has, or the style of the wheels on my vehicle. Those are not the things that define a life of faith. When our hearts are aligned with His will, those details become secondary. We might choose something bold or outlandish simply because we like it, not because we are disconnected from God, but because we are walking in the freedom He has given us.

What if we let the fresh waters of God's grace flow freely into our lives, washing away the weights that hold us back? Imagine standing by a river, holding a heavy rock you've carried for years. You feel its weight pressing into your hands, but as you step closer to the water, you hear a gentle invitation: "Let it go." You hesitate, wondering if you'll feel empty without it, but then you release the rock and watch as the current moves it away. The relief is immediate. In my life, I've experienced moments like this, whether in prayer or quiet reflection, where releasing my burdens to God brought an undeniable sense of freedom and lightness.

The Trap of Comparison

Comparison is one of the most subtle yet destructive burdens we carry, and it often stems from the same striving we discussed earlier. It creeps in quietly, influencing how we see ourselves and others.

Comparison truly steals our joy by shifting our focus away from what God has given us and placing it on what others have.

> *"Each one should test their own actions. Then they can take pride in themselves alone, without comparing themselves to someone else."*
> *Galatians 6:4*

Comparison tricks us into believing that our worth is tied to how well we measure up to others. We look at their lives, their achievements, their families, and we start to wonder: Am I enough? Am I doing enough?

For me, this burden showed up in my marriage and parenting. I felt that if my home wasn't in perfect order, if my children didn't behave a certain way, or if my husband didn't meet my expectations, then I was failing. Also, I was comparing my life to what I thought others had, and often felt I wasn't doing enough. Not only that, but I would feel a deep sense of discouragement. So I constantly pushed myself to ensure everything was orderly, which was especially challenging with four children. This sense of unworthiness often made me irritable and impatient with my family, creating a cycle that felt impossible to break.

Over time, I began to let go of the pressure to have a perfectly tidy house, realizing I had been using it as a measure of my worth. I still love a clean, organized house, but I'm learning to embrace the imperfections without cringing when someone visits and it's messy. Releasing that pressure has helped me be more present with my family and embrace daily imperfections.

This constant comparison left me feeling inadequate and drained, but understanding God's perspective brought relief and clarity. It was as if I had been running a race I could never win, measuring myself against an ever-changing standard. What helped me was understanding that God wasn't looking at how clean, orderly, or organized my house was, or whether my children were perfectly behaved. I also realized that my husband's perceived failures were not mine to fix; they were his. All I needed to do was work on myself. I had to remind myself that his problems were not mine to carry. Letting go of what I mistakenly thought were my duties as a wife freed me to focus on my own growth, trusting that as I leaned on God, the rest would come into place.

God doesn't ask us to measure our worth against others. He asks us to walk the path He has set before us, trusting that it's uniquely designed for our growth and His glory. Comparison isn't a measure of faithfulness; it's a distraction.

Burdens You Were Never Meant to Carry

Some burdens are simply part of living in a broken world. Health challenges, financial struggles, or caring for loved ones are realities we face. But there are the burdens we take on unnecessarily—the ones that weigh us down without purpose or benefit.

> *"Cast all your anxiety on him because he cares for you."*   *1 Peter 5:7*

Jesus invites us to cast our burdens on Him, yet we often cling to them out of habit or fear. *What if letting go means losing control? What if the weight we've carried for so long is all we know?*

I've realized that many of the burdens I carried (perfectionism, control, and a constant need for approval) were never placed on me by God. These were weights I picked up on my own, believing they were necessary to prove my worth or fulfill my role. For years, I placed impossible expectations on myself and my family, thinking their behaviors were a reflection of my worth. If my children misbehaved or my husband didn't meet my standards, I felt like a failure. This mindset didn't just burden me—it burdened them, too.

Among the burdens I carried, perfectionism was one of the heaviest. It whispered that I had to do all the things to be worthy. This constant striving left me feeling disconnected from my family and distant from the peace I longed for. But over time, God showed me that my worth isn't tied to what I do; it's tied to who I am in Him.

Perfectionism is a master deceiver. It tells us that if we just try harder, do more, and be better, we can finally achieve the approval and fulfillment we're longing for. But this is a lie. It doesn't bring peace, it brings exhaustion. And it robs us of the joy and freedom that Jesus came to give.

> *"For it is by grace you have been saved, through faith—and this is not from yourselves, it is the gift of God."*   *Ephesians 2:8*

Letting go of burdens isn't easy. It requires unlearning deeply ingrained habits and replacing them with trust in God's provision and plan. But He never intended for us to carry these heavy loads.

His way is one of grace, inviting us into peace and the freedom to live fully as His beloved.

Shining the Light of Joy

Shining our light comes from the deep understanding of what Jesus spared us from. A thankfulness that comes from the recess of our hearts because we knew we were a lost cause without Him. Calmness comes from knowing who we belong to and the kind of power we have through Him.

What would it look like to carry joy instead of burdens? To let God's peace and love radiate from your life, even in the midst of difficulty? Jesus calls us to live with joy in our hearts, though I know I don't always live this out as well as I'd like.

When things feel chaotic or out of control, taking a deep breath and reminding myself that God is in control has helped me find peace. Sometimes I need to step away briefly to regain peace and perspective, allowing myself to refocus on what truly matters and hold onto the joy God wants me to shine. If things get heated, saying, "Let me come back to you on this," can help keep me from losing the joy I want to share with the world.

"The joy of the Lord is your strength."
Nehemiah 8:10

Witnessing someone truly embody joy becomes especially apparent when they navigate a stressful situation with calmness and grace. It's not always easy to remain calm when things are not going well, but witnessing joy in action inspires me. It is my desire to carry that same joy as a reflection of Jesus in me.

Joy isn't the absence of struggle; it's the assurance of God's presence in the midst of it. This assurance doesn't mean life will always be easy, but it reminds us that we are never alone and that God's grace is sufficient for every moment. When we trust Him with our burdens, we become living testimonies of His grace and faithfulness.

A Personal Journey of Unburdening

Growing up, I watched my parents struggle with burdens tied to their faith. My dad held tightly to the traditions he'd been taught in his plain, Mennonite upbringing (a different church group than the Holdeman Mennonites) while my mom came from a very different world. She was raised in Paraguay, where her parents worked hard to provide for their family. They weren't rich, but they lived simply, making the most of what they had. Manioca, a staple crop, was considered a necessity. Every family had some growing, and if they didn't, they were considered the poorest of the poor. My mom's parents weren't particularly religious, though they had their own code of proper conduct. She now has siblings who are believers and practice the teachings of Jesus.

My dad's parents had moved to Paraguay for religious reasons. As a teenager, my mom went to work for them, and somewhere along the way, she and my dad fell in love. They married when she was just sixteen, beginning a new life together within the structured traditions of his community.

Though my parents came from very different upbringings, both carried deeply held beliefs about faith and how it should be lived out. They also came from large families—my mom, the oldest; my dad, the youngest. The contrast in their backgrounds, along with my mom's young age, brought challenges into their relationship. I believe it would have for anyone.

Life can be difficult even when you grow up in the same community with shared practices because every family has its own ideas of what is right, what is too much or not enough, and where the line between right and wrong should be drawn. Looking back, I can appreciate how hard it must have been for both of my parents. It isn't easy to yield to something that doesn't feel true to you. Despite their sincere efforts, it often felt like there was bondage instead of freedom. They sought to pass these traditions on to us, and while some of their teachings strengthened our character, others hindered us from fully embracing the freedom Jesus offers.

It took me time to separate what was truly rooted in faith from what was simply a weight passed down from generation to generation. Learning to embrace that freedom has been a journey of unlearning and trusting that God's grace is greater than tradition.

> *"Then you will know the truth, and the truth will set you free."*   *John 8:32*

Because of how my parents taught us and the misconceptions I acquired through different people and the community, I carried burdens that weighed me down. I had accepted Jesus as my Savior, but over time, I gradually added burdens to what He had already taken care of. These burdens were tied to performance and perfection.

As I've grown, I've recognized how these patterns influenced me. I carried these burdens, believing my worth was tied to how well I conformed to expectations. But over time, God has been teaching me to let go—unburdening, in a sense—by releasing the need to perform, the drive for perfection, and the belief that I was unworthy of love.

I always thought of love as conditional, something to be earned. But God's love is unconditional, and for that, I am deeply grateful.

The unburdening process isn't a one-time event—it's a daily choice to surrender. It's like a backpack loaded with things you don't need. As time passes, you take out the unnecessary items, and little by little, your load becomes lighter. It requires extending grace to myself and others, trusting that God is working all things for good.

> *"Do not conform to the pattern of this world, but be transformed by the renewing of your mind."*
> *Romans 12:2*

Renewing our minds is transformative; it reshapes how we see life and ourselves. It made all the difference for me to start thinking differently about life and myself. We have been challenged to look in the mirror and tell ourselves we are beautiful, not by the world's standards, but by God's. Renewing our minds means challenging the beliefs and patterns that keep us stuck. It means asking hard questions: Why am I holding onto this? What am I afraid of losing if I let it go?

An Invitation to Freedom

As you reflect on this chapter, I invite you to consider your own burdens. What are you carrying today that God might be asking you to release?

"Do not be anxious about anything, but in every situation, by prayer and petition, with thanksgiving, present your requests to God. And the peace of God, which transcends all understanding, will guard your hearts and minds in Christ Jesus" (Philippians 4:6-7). Unburdening your load isn't about abandoning responsibility; it's about trusting God to carry what you cannot. It's about exchanging the weight of guilt, comparison, and perfectionism for the freedom, joy, and peace that only He can provide.

Jesus invites you to walk with Him, lay your burdens at His feet, and experience the rest your soul longs for. His invitation isn't just for today, it's for every step of your journey. Will you take Him up on that offer to lay down your burdens and walk in His lasting peace and joy?

Reflection Questions:

1. What burdens are you carrying right now that feel too heavy to bear? Take a moment to identify which ones you might be holding onto unnecessarily.

2. How has comparison or perfectionism influenced the way you see yourself, your family, or your faith? What would it look like to let go of these pressures?

3. What step can you take today to surrender your burdens to Jesus and experience the rest He promises?

CHAPTER 7

Experiencing God Through Nature

> *"I love to think of nature as an unlimited broadcasting station, through which God speaks to us every hour, if we will only tune in."[6]*
> —*George Washington Carver*

The Beauty of Creation

Walking in nature fills me with a deep sense of God's presence. Every sunrise and sunset feels like a personal message from Him. The vibrant colors of flowers, the expanse of blue skies, and the radiant sunlight all point to His majesty. Even the stars at night declare the glory of a Creator who not only made them but named them (Psalm 147:4). How humbling it is to realize that this same God, who knows when a sparrow falls and counts the hairs on our heads (Matthew 10:29–30), cares deeply for you and me.

As you step outside, let nature draw your mind to God. The elaborate beauty of His creation is a reflection of His love for us. If He invested so much care in creating the world, imagine the masterpiece He is shaping in you. Philippians 1:6 assures us that "...he

---

6   Direct citation is not available. Concepts aligned with information found by George Washington Carver.

who began a good work in you will carry it on to completion..." God's plan for you is intentional and full of purpose.

Take a moment to observe the small details—the way dew glistens on grass, the gentle rustling of leaves in the wind, or the sound of birds singing their morning praises. Each of these moments is an invitation to pause and recognize God's intricate design. Psalm 19:1 says, "The heavens declare the glory of God; the skies proclaim the work of his hands." Let these details inspire gratitude and wonder in your heart.

Trusting God's Guidance

God invites us to trust Him completely. When we place our hand in His, we acknowledge our desire for Him to lead us. There will be days when relinquishing control feels difficult, but the truth is, we have limited control over external circumstances. What we can control are our thoughts and actions, and these must align with the path God sets before us.

Proverbs 3:5–6 reminds us, "Trust in the Lord with all your heart and lean not on your own understanding; in all your ways submit to him, and he will make your paths straight." Let God's peace guide you as you grow in Christlikeness, surrendering your worries to Him. When challenges arise, remember that He is your constant companion. Isaiah 41:10 assures us, "So do not fear, for I am with you; do not be dismayed, for I am your God. I will strengthen you and help you; I will uphold you with my righteous right hand."

How beautiful and wonderful it is to know we have all these promises from God! He will help us and wants to be a constant presence in our lives.

I love remembering what it felt like to stand at the edge of the ocean watching the waves roll in. The sounds of the waves surrounded me, and in that moment, I felt an overwhelming sense of peace. It was as if God was speaking to me through the vastness of the ocean, reminding me to trust Him with every part of my life. If He could command this great expanse of water, how much more could He sustain and support me? What is amazing to me is that I feel this every time I stop to watch and listen to the waves.

It's a beautiful reminder of how deeply God cares for me. In the vastness of nature, or even in the smallest detail like a dewdrop, His presence shines through as a testament to His love and care for all of creation. If He takes the time to craft such exquisite details in nature, how much more does He cherish and care for you?

Awe-Inspiring Travels

Road trips can be challenging due to the long hours, restless children, and unexpected detours, but they are also immensely rewarding. For me, the opportunity to see nature's wonders, which so clearly point to a Creator whose works are unfathomable, makes it all worth it. Last summer, our family ventured out on a journey to Montana, and it became a trip filled with so much awe, gratitude, and reflection.

Traveling to Montana felt like a dream come true. As a teenager, I was captivated by the idea of visiting this vast, rugged state, though I never truly believed it would happen. It was a dream tucked away in the background of my mind, one I thought would remain there. Reading books about Montana had intrigued me—its mountains, open skies, and unspoiled landscapes seemed otherworldly. When we finally made the decision to take this trip, I couldn't contain my eagerness to begin our travels.

To make it more special, we chose a scenic route, allowing us to savor the journey as much as the destination. What made this trip even more meaningful was the chance to travel across the country with our children. They were old enough to enjoy and make memories of the trip, and sharing those experiences together was a blessing. From moments of fun and laughter to quiet reflection on the beauty surrounding us, it was a journey I will always cherish.

Arkansas: A Historical and Natural State

We left the flatlands of the Mississippi Delta and crossed the mighty Mississippi River into Arkansas. Our first stop was Little Rock, where we stayed the night. The next morning, we visited a state park to purchase a pass for the National Parks—our gateway to countless adventures. While our stop in Little Rock was brief, it left an impression. The landscape—a mix of rolling hills and verdant forests—was a refreshing change from the flat delta lands. My insatiable desire to know more about history stirred as I thought about the years long passed, the stories these lands might hold, and the people who once walked here. Reflecting on this deepened my sense of purpose, reminding me that God weaves history, both the past and my own, into His greater plan. I was also struck by the area's rich history. Though I would have loved to explore it further, we were focused on the natural wonders ahead.

Even at this early point of our journey, I felt a sense of anticipation. The surrounding beauty hinted at what was to come, and I couldn't help but reflect on the Creator who had crafted it all. As we left Arkansas, I prayed for our trip to be filled with moments that would draw us closer as a family and closer to God—a gift I want to always remember.

Oklahoma: A Visit with Love

Our next stop was in Oklahoma, where we visited Terry's great-aunt. She was a sweet, gentle woman who exuded love and kindness. My children adored her, and her warm hospitality left a lasting impression on all of us. Though we hadn't spent much time with her in the past, her presence made us feel cherished. She exemplified the fruit of the Spirit: "love, joy, peace, patience, kindness, goodness, faithfulness, gentleness, and self-control" (Galatians 5:22-23). She radiated a beautiful spirit, and you just wanted to be near her. What a testimony to leave behind.

Looking back, I am so grateful we made the effort to visit her. She passed away just a few months later, and knowing we had that precious time with her brings me comfort. This experience reminded me of the importance of prioritizing relationships. Work, projects, and responsibilities can wait, but the time we have with loved ones is fleeting. It's worth going out of your way to show someone you care.

Texas: Hidden Gems in the Desert

From Oklahoma, we made our way into Texas, stopping for the night in Amarillo. The next morning, we detoured about 30 minutes south to visit Palo Duro Canyon State Park. Often referred to as the "Grand Canyon of Texas," this park exceeded our expectations. The vibrant red and orange cliffs stood in stark contrast to the blue sky, and the sprawling views seemed to stretch forever.

As we explored the canyon, I marveled at the Creator's handiwork. Each layer of rock told a story of time and transformation, reminding me of how God shapes our lives through seasons of change. Standing at the edge of the canyon, I felt small yet deeply connected to something greater than myself. My children were delighted by the adventure, and so were we. We decided that we were catching glimpses of what the Grand Canyon in Arizona would have to offer if we ever got the chance to go. On our way out, we stopped at a mercantile called The Sad Monkey to get some coffee drinks. Coffee stops have become a tradition for us—perhaps not the most practical habit, given the cost, but it's one of those special things we enjoy doing with our children. I love making memories, and those spontaneous stops are one way of doing this.

Colorado: Sand Dunes and Majesty

Crossing into Colorado, we were greeted by an entirely different landscape. Our first major stop was at the Great Sand Dunes National Park. The sight of these towering dunes, surrounded by snow-capped mountains, was breathtaking. It felt like we had entered another world. It's hard to put into words the overwhelming feeling of being surrounded by such magnificence, a reminder of God's unfathomable creativity and power.

Climbing the dunes was no easy task. With each step, our feet sank into the soft sand, making progress slow and laborious. The heat of the day added to the challenge, but reaching the top of some of the lower dunes was worth every effort. From our vantage point, we could see the vast expanse of dunes stretching out before us, framed by the rugged peaks of the Sangre de Cristo Mountains.

Life can feel like climbing those dunes. Some challenges take more effort than we expect, and the journey can be slow and frustrating. But the struggle, perseverance, and willingness to keep moving forward—it's always worth it. Even if we don't reach the highest peak, the view from where we stand can still be breathtaking

We didn't try climbing to the tops of the sand dunes—it would have taken a lot of time. As we stood there, we acknowledged that if, for whatever reason, the sand shifted or the wind changed, it was possible we could get covered and lost in the sand. It was a sobering thought, but also another one of those moments where we said, "Wow, God, what a wonder You have created."

As I reflected later, Psalm 8:3–4 came to mind: "When I consider your heavens, the work of your fingers, the moon and the stars, which you have set in place, what is mankind that you are mindful of them, human beings that you care for them?"

This verse has always been a source of awe for me. It reminds me of how vast and intricate God's creation is, yet He still cares deeply for each of us. Standing atop the dunes and gazing at the surrounding mountains, I felt the truth of these words in a new way—that the same God who painted the heavens and shaped the earth also knows me by name. Standing there, I felt a deep sense of wonder and humility. The God who created this vast, intricate landscape also created me—a small but significant part of His marvelous creation.

We slid back down the dunes, eager to escape the heat of the day, but filled with gratitude for the opportunity to experience such beauty. Tired and ready for a break, we noticed the sand had found its way into every corner of our shoes. Moments like these reminded me of the joy that comes from simply being together and marveling at God's creation, even while experiencing the discomfort of heat and sand in our shoes.

New Mexico: The Beauty of Transition

Leaving Colorado, we briefly passed through the eastern corner of New Mexico. The landscape began to shift from green forests to red, rugged terrain. One outstanding landmark was Shiprock, a massive rock formation that resembles a ship sailing through the desert. Its striking beauty was captivating, and it served as a reminder of how diverse God's creation is. Each new region brought its own special beauty, a reflection of the Creator's boundless imagination. It never ceases to amaze me, witnessing the incredible diversity and the unfathomable splendor of His magnificent creation. We stopped at

The Four Corners, a place where the incredible diversity of creation is on full display. It was truly awe-inspiring, and I am so grateful we had the chance to experience it together. Moments like these remind me how blessed we are to witness the wonder of God's handiwork firsthand.

Mesa Verde: A Glimpse into the Past

Our next stop was Mesa Verde National Park in Colorado. This park is home to the ancient cliff dwellings of the Ancestral Puebloans, a testament to human ingenuity and resilience. As we drove higher and higher up the winding mountain roads, the views grew increasingly breathtaking. At one overlook, we paused to take it all in—the green valleys below, the distant peaks, and the intricate dwellings carved into the cliffs.

Exploring Mesa Verde felt like stepping back in time. I couldn't help but marvel at how these early inhabitants lived in harmony with their environment, using the surrounding resources to create thriving communities. Their story reminded me of the importance of adaptability and resourcefulness, qualities that God equips us with to navigate life's challenges.

Utah: Arches National Park

From Mesa Verde, we continued our journey to Arches National Park in Utah. This extraordinary park was a feast for the senses, with its vivid red and orange rock formations, dramatic arches, and sweeping vistas. Each structure seemed impossibly balanced, as though defying gravity itself. The colors, textures, and sheer scale of the landscape left us utterly in awe. Driving through the park, I found myself in a constant state of amazement, my mouth frequently dropping open as I whispered, "Wow." Everywhere we looked, the formations seemed to defy reality, each a masterpiece of design.

Walking among the arches, I was struck by how time and pressure had shaped these rocks into such magnificent forms. It was as though God's hand had carefully woven together the elements of wind, water, and time to create these breathtaking landscapes. Each curve and arch told a story of resilience and transformation, shaped by the forces around it but always held together by an invisible thread of purpose.

This imagery reminded me of how God weaves our lives with the same intricate care. Through the challenges, hardships, and pressures we face, He is creating something beautiful and strong within us. Just as the arches stand as enduring symbols of grace and strength, our lives are being woven into a masterpiece by the Master Weaver. Every thread—whether one of joy or sorrow—is part of the larger design, a design we may not always see clearly but one that is always crafted with love.

Standing under one of the massive arches, I felt a profound sense of peace and reassurance. If the God who wove together such awe-inspiring landscapes cared enough to form every curve and balance, how much more must He care for me? The arches were a vivid reminder that I am part of His divine tapestry, held together by His grace and shaped with purpose.

This thought filled me with hope and a deeper trust in His plan. The shaping of the arches took centuries, enduring relentless forces, but the result is nothing short of spectacular. In the same way, the pressures and trials we face may feel overwhelming, but they are the threads God uses to create something extraordinary in our lives.

Arches National Park became more than a destination on our trip; it became a testament to God's creative power and His boundless love. As I remember standing under those incredible formations, I am reminded that the same God who shaped together the arches with such care is weaving my life with the same intention. Truly, the God who created such magnificence also holds us in His hands, weaving a story of hope, grace, and love.

Idaho and Montana: The Journey's Culmination

Leaving Utah, we headed into Idaho, a state of towering mountains and vibrant green trees that seemed to glow under the sunlight. The air felt crisp and refreshing, a reminder of how alive nature makes you feel. We stayed the night with a new friend I had met earlier that summer in Texas. She welcomed us warmly, and it was a delight to share stories and laughter before continuing our journey. It was one of those beautiful connections that only come because of God.

The next day, we set our sights on Yellowstone, a place I had always dreamed of visiting. It was another one of those "I-can't-believe-this-is-happening" moments. Yellowstone was more incredible than I could have imagined. From geysers shooting into the sky to herds of elk grazing peacefully, the park was a living portrait of God's creativity and majesty. We were fortunate to see both Old Faithful and a lesser-known geyser called Honeybee erupt. My brother and his family joined us, making the experience even more special.

The sky was an unbroken expanse of brilliant blue, and the air was so clean it felt invigorating to breathe. Every detail in the park, from the bubbling hot springs to the vibrant wildflowers, spoke of an awesome Creator. God's fingerprints were everywhere. I couldn't stop marveling at how everything pointed back to Him and His love for us. To think that the same God who created this awe-inspiring park also knows and loves me personally was overwhelming.

By evening, we arrived at my brother's home in Montana. As we had crossed into Montana, I felt a strange and comforting sense of belonging, as though I were coming home. Montana was everything I had dreamed it would be, and so much more. The drive there was as stunning as every other part of the trip. Towering mountains, rugged and snow-capped, framed the horizon. The sense of vastness and beauty made me feel small, yet deeply connected to the Creator. As we pulled into my brother's driveway, I was so grateful that we could experience all of this with our children.

Experiencing God's Presence Through Nature and Travel

This trip was filled with moments of wonder, beauty, and reflection. Each destination reinforced the truth that God's creation is a testament to His love and greatness. Whether it was the Bonneville Salt Flats, the shifting sands of the dunes, or the vibrant sunsets, nature continually pointed us back to Him.

Travel also offered lessons in adaptability and gratitude. Moments of detours, delays, and exhaustion were overshadowed by the joy of discovery and the memories we created. Psalm 23:3 reminds us, "He refreshes my soul. He guides me along the right paths for his name's sake." As we drove through winding mountain roads and walked among towering peaks, these words resonated deeply. Each turn and every view brought renewal, as though God Himself was inviting me to slow down, breathe deeply, and trust His guidance.

This journey wasn't just about physical beauty; it was about the peace that came from knowing He was leading every step of the way. How beautiful it is to walk with the Lord, to witness His hand in every detail of creation, and to experience His refreshment and guidance.

Returning home, I carried with me a renewed sense of awe for God's creation and a deeper appreciation for time spent with family. This trip was more than a road trip; it was a reminder of the Creator's presence in every detail, from grand landscapes to quiet moments of connection. Truly, God is good.

Through every mountain, canyon, and starry night, God's message is clear: He loves us deeply. Let His creation draw you closer to Him and remind you of His faithfulness.

"Be still, and know that I am God." Psalm 46:10

In the stillness of nature, may you find His peace and presence.

By embracing God's masterpiece in nature, we can find grounding and renewal. Walking outside, even briefly, lightens burdens and shifts perspectives. Just as God designed the natural world to function in harmony, He has a plan for each of us. Caring for our bodies and minds honors the Creator who designed us.

As I reflect on this journey, I am filled with gratitude for the memories created and the lessons learned. Every moment, whether basking in the grandeur of nature or sharing quiet times of connection, reinforced a profound truth: we are deeply loved by a God who cares about every detail of our lives.

It is my hope and prayer that you, too, find inspiration in God's creation and experience the depth of His unconditional love. This is not a love that you must earn or strive for; it is a love that meets you exactly where you are, a love that has no limits or conditions. Just as the mountains stand steadfast, and the rivers flow freely, so does God's love for you remain constant and unshaken.

In every sunrise, He whispers, "I see you." In every gentle breeze, He reminds you, "I am with you." And in the quiet stillness of your heart, He assures you, "You are mine." The same God who crafted the wonders of the world also crafted you, with care, intention, and a purpose only you can fulfill.

Let this truth fill you with hope: You are not forgotten. You are not lost in the vastness of creation. Instead, you are cherished, uniquely chosen, and fully known. God's love is not reserved for the perfect, the accomplished, or the strong—it is for all of us, in every season, in every state. His arms are always open, inviting you to rest in His presence and trust in His goodness.

May you find peace in knowing that He has a place for you, a purpose intricately woven into the fabric of your life. Whether you are walking through a season of joy or navigating a time of uncertainty, He is with you, guiding you, and calling you closer to Him.

My desire for you, dear reader, is that you embrace this love with open arms. Allow it to transform your heart, heal your wounds, and fill your life with a renewed sense of hope. Just as the beauty of creation reflects His glory, your life reflects His grace. Walk confidently in that love, knowing that it is unconditional, unending, and always enough.

Reflection Questions:

1. What is one moment from your travels or daily life where you felt deeply connected to God's creation? How did that moment shape your understanding of His presence in your life?

2. What are some ways you can prioritize creating meaningful memories with your loved ones, even during busy or challenging seasons?

3. How do you see God's hand in the diversity and beauty of the world around you? In what ways does this inspire gratitude or awe in your daily life?

CHAPTER 8

Rest in His Love

"I rest, Lord, in your unfailing love."
—Psalm 6:4, (adapted)

Embracing the Gift of God's Love

Have you ever considered what it truly means to rest in God's love? It's one thing to know about His love, but another to fully embrace it. Do you know God, the One who created love itself? Do you know Jesus, who gave His life because He loves you so profoundly? Resting in His love could be as simple as imagining the embrace of someone you hold dear or the warmth of holding a sleeping child in your arms. A child is completely dependent on someone else to care for them, and in many ways, that is how we are with God. He is our ultimate caregiver, meeting our every need with His unfailing love.

For many, grasping the depth of God's love isn't easy. I know because it took me years to truly understand how much God loves me, and I really can't say that I actually understand it deeply enough even now. There was a time in my life when I felt overwhelmed by failure, unable to see past my shortcomings. Yet, in that season, God's love shone through in unexpected ways: a kind word from a friend, a Scripture that spoke directly to my heart, or an unexplainable sense of peace that calmed my fears. Reflecting on those moments, I began to realize that His love is not conditional on my performance; it is steadfast and unchanging.

You must see God's love for you and take it in with your whole heart. Can you imagine being loved so completely that your mistakes don't define you? That's the kind of love God offers, a love that says, "You are mine, and nothing will change that." Even if you sin, you are still loved as if you hadn't done a thing. God is love, and He also hates sin, but because of Jesus, you can rest in His everlasting, unconditional love—love that covers you completely.

Romans 8:38–39 says, "For I am convinced that neither death nor life, neither angels nor demons, neither the present nor the future, nor any powers, neither height nor depth, nor anything else in all creation, will be able to separate us from the love of God that is in Christ Jesus our Lord." Imagine living with the assurance of this unbreakable love; it is life-changing. It's that overwhelming sense of peace, safety, and assurance. He is in it all.

Resting in God's love is going to bed each night knowing He has been with you throughout the day, even in your struggles. It's trusting that, through your imperfections, He sees your heart and loves you still. His love is all-encompassing, far beyond what we can fully understand. It is a magnificent love, and I encourage you to accept it.

What Does It Mean to Rest in His Love?

Resting in His love means surrendering every part of our lives to Him. But sometimes, we unknowingly limit God. Have you ever asked yourself, How big is my God? Do I trust Him with everything, or do I still try to manage parts of my life on my own?

Reflecting on my journey, I see how learning to trust in God's great love has been a process, one marked by growth, setbacks, and revelations. I remember a specific moment during a particularly challenging season in my life. I was facing uncertainties that left me feeling overwhelmed and fearful. One evening, as I prayed, a sense of peace washed over me, a peace that could only come from God. I've encountered other moments like this, and it's been a gradual turning point, reminding me that His love is steadfast even in my darkest days. It was then that I began to see how surrendering to His love allowed me to grow in trust and faith. It helps us to remember those moments when God shows up for us; it's often far more frequent than we realize if we take the time to notice.

God longs for us to attend His classroom of life. It's not because He wants to teach us a thing or two, but rather as an invitation to see what He has to offer if we are willing to learn from Him. He invites us to lay down our burdens and rest in Him.

> *"Cast all your anxiety on Him because He cares for you."*   *1 Peter 5:7*

Many of us struggle to fully trust Him. I am not saying it is easy to trust, but when you stop and take notice, you will see the pattern that unfolds and God working behind the scenes. Sometimes His work is hidden, but often enough it is in full display, leaving no doubt that it was Him. These moments remind us that He cares deeply for every detail of our lives and invites us to lean into His faithfulness. I know people who call them "God moments" because there is nothing else that could explain it.

Do you keep a mental record of all the times God has shown up in your life? There was a season in my life when I would go to church and wonder if I was God's child—was I on track? During the course of the week, I would read something or share a thought with someone. Then on Sundays in the sermon, the minister would make reference to that exact thought I had or connect with the reading I had read. To me, it was a confirmation. It was as though God Himself was saying, "I see you, and I am here. You are on track and I love you." Those moments reminded me that God shows up in both big and small ways if we're paying attention. It's a practice, but once you start, you will wonder why you didn't begin sooner.

When you take time to pay attention, you might be amazed at His faithfulness. He is in the large things of our lives as well as in the small ones. And sometimes, His love appears in the smallest, quietest ways, like a solution to a problem, a word of encouragement, or an indescribable peace. Begin looking for those moments, and you will be well on your way to trusting to rest in His love. It will become a real life-giving transformation.

Trusting God with All Areas of Your Life

If you're unsure of your faith in God, consider this: You are already putting your faith in something, even if it's yourself. True peace comes from believing in God's love, a foundation that cannot be shaken. As Isaiah 26:3 says, "You will keep in perfect peace those whose minds are steadfast, because they trust in you."

I know you must believe in God for His promises to mean anything to you. I like to believe that whoever picks up this book and reads it already believes in God; you just need to be encouraged to trust Him completely.

In the past, I believed that God only cared about my spirituality. That's what I thought I needed to focus on. If there was trouble, I assumed it was because I wasn't spiritual enough. But that isn't true. God cares about every part of our being. Our spiritual, emotional, mental, and physical health are interconnected, signaling how we are doing overall. Focusing only on one area creates an unbalanced life, making it harder to trust and rest in God's love. For example, neglecting our physical health can lead to an unhealthy body, or ignoring emotional needs can strain relationships. Trusting God with all areas means surrendering every part of our lives to His care, knowing He wants us to thrive in every way.

You must trust God with everything, inviting Him into every part, your joys, struggles, and even the parts you try to handle on your own. His love extends to every detail of who you are, and He longs to guide you into a balanced and abundant life.

> *"Take my yoke upon you and learn from me, for I am gentle and humble in heart, and you will find rest for your souls. For my yoke is easy, and my burden is light."*　　　　　　　　　　Matthew 11:29–30

As you read this verse, what are your thoughts? Often, I feel like my yoke is hard, and my burdens are heavy. But what I believe this verse is saying is not that life will be without difficulty, but that Jesus makes my yoke easy and my burden light because He carries it with me. The full weight of what we are dealing with is lightened because of Him. It's a beautiful exchange, our struggles for His strength, our fears for His peace.

God's Guiding Hand

Learning to rest in God's love isn't just about understanding it—it's about experiencing it. There have been countless times in my life when I had to trust His love in the middle of uncertainty. One of those times was when my family and I planned a trip to Paraguay. Most of my mom's family lived there, including her mother and siblings. Since our last visit over five years earlier, my grandfather, my mom's dad, had passed away. As we planned the trip, we looked forward to reconnecting with her family and spending time with loved ones we hadn't seen in years.

We planned our visit for over Christmas, and we were going to stay for three weeks. Our journey began with a drive to Miami, where we would catch a direct flight to Asunción. This trip took place in 2012, and as of now, it remains the last time we've been to Paraguay.

Lately, my children have been saying it's time for another trip, and I agree with them. My youngest is ten and has never been there. It feels like we need to take time to go back, to reconnect with family and share that part of my heritage with her.

Two weeks before arriving in Paraguay, I had to fly to Miami to see why my passport wasn't being renewed. I drove two and a half hours to Jackson, Mississippi, to catch a flight to Miami. Upon arriving, I took a taxi to the Paraguayan embassy, where I was informed that I would need to travel to Paraguay to resolve the issue. They also provided me with a document explaining why I was traveling without a passport. My passport had been delayed in Asunción due to mismatched information between their records and mine in the state. Despite the challenges, I know God was with me in those moments, helping me find a ticket, make that drive to Jackson, and accomplish all of this in just one day. This was just the beginning of a journey where I would see God's hand guiding me every step of the way.

Arriving in Paraguay, I encountered yet another moment where God's guiding hand was unmistakable. From the challenges I faced in Miami to the moments in Paraguay, the thread of His presence was woven through it all. What should have been a drawn-out, weeks-long process was resolved in just two days. With my limited understanding of Spanish, I managed to explain my situation to a taxi driver. By chance, or divine intervention, as it turned out, he was well-acquainted with the chief of police, and he happened to be the one we got into his car. I remember sitting in the back seat of the cab, explaining my situation, and he offered to go in and speak with him. By the end of the day, my passport was well on its way to being renewed, a process that had felt almost impossible. Looking back, I see the unmistakable touch of God's guidance throughout that experience.

Right after receiving my passport, Terry and I caught the bus to meet up with our family at the bustling outdoor market in Asunción. We had no way to contact my family, and I felt a rising sense of panic, wondering how we would ever reconnect. It was as if I had subconsciously uttered a prayer, though I didn't speak the words aloud. Moments later, we spotted my daughter and brother crossing the street, a wave of relief washing over me. I knew God was in that moment, just as He had been throughout the trip. This moment felt like a continuation of God's guidance throughout the entire journey, from the initial hurdles in Miami to the gentle mercies in Asunción. From navigating the complexities of renewing my passport to this seemingly small but significant reunion, I was reminded that God's hand is present in both the major hurdles and the subtle, gentle mercies of our lives.

> *"Trust in the Lord with all your heart and lean not on your own understanding in all your ways submit to Him, and He will make your paths straight."*
> Proverbs 3:5–6

This scripture encourages us to trust in God rather than relying on ourselves, a promise we can lean on and hold close. It reminds us that God will guide us toward His purpose, leading us to His perfect plan. And because of His unconditional love, He is always waiting for us to turn to Him with our needs. Even when we don't understand the path ahead, we can rest in knowing that He sees the bigger picture and will make our paths straight.

Overcoming Barriers to Rest

Resting in His love also requires attention to your thoughts.

> *"Do not conform to the pattern of this world, but be transformed by the renewing of your mind."*
> *Romans 12:2*

Your thought patterns have profound power. I know this first-hand. When I fixated on my failures and shortcomings, it was all I could see. I realized over time how often I focused on my mistakes and how this mindset consumed me. It wasn't a single moment, but rather a gradual understanding that God didn't require me to beat myself up over my failures. He began showing me that while I needed to admit when I messed up, I could trust in His grace rather than live in constant self-condemnation. Over time, I started to see things differently; resting in His love meant embracing His grace and letting go of the perfection I was chasing. Being so fixated on my shortcomings clouded my ability to recognize God's presence and grace in my life. It was a hindrance to accepting and resting in His love.

Accepting His love transforms how we see ourselves and others. His love is not earned, it is freely given. But receiving it requires faith.

> *"And without faith, it is impossible to please God..."*
> *Hebrews 11:6*

Belief in His promises is the gateway to experiencing the fullness of His love.

Recognizing God's Presence in Everyday Life

I know some people struggle with the idea of God's love when their circumstances seem dire. Why does suffering exist? Why does God allow pain, especially for the innocent? These are hard questions, and while we may not understand why suffering exists, we can trust that God's love remains constant, even in the midst of our pain.

> *"'For my thoughts are not your thoughts, neither are your ways my ways,' declares the Lord."* Isaiah 55:8

This is a stumbling block for many. People say, "If God is loving, why doesn't He stop all the pain and suffering?" It's a valid question, but it often stems from misunderstanding what a loving God truly is. Love doesn't control; it frees. God gave every human the power of choice, a gift that allows for genuine love but also the possibility of pain. Forced love isn't love at all.

This struggle with understanding love isn't just about how we see God—it also shapes how we experience love in our own relationships.

Forced love will never give you the deep connection you long for. Love, by its very nature, must be freely given to thrive. When we require someone to meet certain expectations in order to receive our love, whether through behaviors, words, or actions, we are not truly loving them. Instead, we are attempting to control them, tying love to performance rather than allowing it to flow from the heart.

I know this because I've been there. I tried to be perfect in every way—I obsessed over my looks, my weight, and how I presented myself, because deep down, I feared that if I wasn't good enough, my husband could stop loving me. That fear was exhausting. It made me believe that love was something to be maintained through effort, rather than something given freely. And what made it worse? I didn't even realize I had built this expectation myself. Somewhere along the way, through the things I absorbed, the messages I internalized, I created a belief that love had to be earned, that I had to meet a certain standard to be worthy of it.

I had once read that expectations are resentments in the making. That truth hit me, but it took a while before I would truly understand how deeply it applied to my life.

During a time of learning and healing, I had an honest conversation with my husband about not feeling good enough. I shared my fears, insecurities, all the things I thought I had to be in order to keep his love. And to my surprise, he told me he felt the same way—that he was never good enough for me. His words stopped me in my tracks. I had been so focused on meeting expectations that I didn't even realize I had been placing expectations on him as well. Without meaning to, I had been withholding unconditional love from the very person I needed to show it to the most. That realization sank deep. It made me see how deeply expectations had been ingrained in me, how they were shaping not just how I received love, but how I gave it.

But God's love is nothing like that. His love isn't based on what we do, how we look, or whether we meet some impossible standard. He loves us fully, just as we are. When we grasp for love, control it, or try to earn it, we are living out of fear rather than trust. And love rooted in fear is built on a shaky foundation—it will eventually crack under the weight of unmet expectations.

If you find yourself trying to hold onto love by striving, proving, or demanding, ask yourself: Where is this fear coming from? Were you taught that love had to be earned? Do you believe, deep down, that you are worthy of love simply as you are? The answers to these questions often reveal where healing is needed.

The truth is, love—real, God-reflecting love—is never forced. It is not given as a reward or withheld as punishment. It is a choice, a gift, a reflection of the One who loves us freely. When we embrace this truth, we can love others without fear, control, and expectation of repayment. We can love from a place of wholeness rather than need. And in doing so, we reflect the very nature of God himself.

As I worked through these realizations about love, I also started to notice how God's presence was woven into my everyday life. It wasn't just in the grand moments of clarity, but in the small, quiet reminders all around me. The more I paid attention, the more I realized He had been there all along—through every struggle, every joy, and even in the in-between spaces where I once felt alone.

I want to remind you that even amidst the challenges, God's presence surrounds us. He's in the beauty of creation, the kindness of a stranger, and the still, small moments of grace we often overlook. I've found this to be true in my own life as well, though it sometimes takes time to see it clearly.

You are a testament to His love and care. Your very existence reflects His presence, woven into the fabric of everyday life. Have you ever paused to notice those moments? I believe God's love is often revealed in the ordinary, a sunset, a comforting word, or an indescribable sense of peace during chaos.

He is always there, even when we fail to see it. The challenge is to open our eyes and hearts to recognize Him in all things. Take a moment today to reflect on where you've seen His presence, even in the smallest details.

Reframing Pain Through His Love

We live in a world of choices, both our own and those of others. Sometimes the ripple effects of others' decisions cause pain, and it's tempting to blame God. I haven't personally faced a struggle where someone's choice profoundly affected my life, but I have had friends who did. It was a struggle to ask, "God, why did You let this happen?" I probably did ask, but it's not a helpful question. Spending time and energy on the wrong questions can leave us stuck. Instead, focus on finding resources that offer solutions or provide support for navigating pain. God is undoubtedly a source of help, but He also equips people to teach skills and offer tools that make our lives better when it feels like everything is falling apart.

People make bad choices, and others are often left to pick up the pieces. My role in those moments was to be the friend sitting with them, offering support in whatever form was needed. That was what I experienced, and I truly feel God was in it all. I saw God show up for my friends. His presence brought comfort to them in ways I could not have provided, reminding me that He works through us and around us to provide strength and grace.

> "The Lord is close to the brokenhearted and saves those who are crushed in spirit"   *Psalm 34:18*

As hard as it is to watch friends be betrayed and left to fend for themselves, His presence is undeniable, providing strength and grace for me to be there for them. God shows up not just for me, but also for them in powerful ways, bringing comfort and direction that only He could provide.

The Transforming Power of Rest

When we rest in His love, we surrender the need for control. We trust that His ways are higher, and His love for us is unchanging. Resting doesn't mean life will be free of hardships, but it does mean we have a refuge, a safe place to lay our burdens. It's like finding an anchor in the storm, holding firm even when the waves crash around us.

I have seen how God shows up for us. When I was struggling with feeling like a lost child, God showed up with arms comforting me with such love. He knows, and He is my safe place. One time, Terry and I were traveling to pick up a trailer when his truck broke down. We sat there by the side of the road for about two hours waiting for someone to help us. I remembered praying and believing that something was going to work out.

Eventually, someone did stop, took us to a Napa store, and there happened to be a man there who had a wrecked truck with the parts we needed. He took us to the place, gave Terry the tools, and said to leave them at the store for him to retrieve later. Otherwise, we would have had to wait days to get the part and be back on the road. Once again, God showed His faithfulness. He bears our burdens and cares for us. This moment reminded me that God's love isn't just a spiritual concept; it's a practical reality where we can see His hand working in the details of our lives.

Resting in God's love also transforms our perspective. When we stop striving and begin trusting, we start to notice His hand in situations we once viewed as hopeless. It might be as simple as seeing a difficult season as an opportunity for growth, or recognizing His provision in unexpected ways. Over time, you learn to release the pressure of having all the answers and lean into His perfect plan. This shift allows you to find peace, knowing that He is working in every detail of your lives, even when it's hard to see. It reminds you that you are not alone, even when the journey feels overwhelming.

If you're carrying the weight of your struggles, I encourage you to bring them to the One whose love is steadfast.

> *"Come to me, all you who are weary and burdened,*
> *and I will give you rest."* Matt. 11:28

Resting in His love means trusting Him with your whole heart and believing He is working all things together for your good.

Practical Steps to Rest in His Love

As you may already know, I love providing practical ways to apply what you are learning. These steps can help you to implement what you've read and begin to experience the rest that comes from God's unconditional love.

Let these steps guide you closer to the peace that comes from fully resting in His love. Start small, choose one step to focus on today. Maybe it's sitting in stillness for a few minutes or jotting down one thing you're grateful for. Little by little, these actions will help you experience the transformative power of His love.

- **Reflect on God's Promises:** Spend time reading and meditating on Scripture that reminds you of His love and faithfulness. Consider keeping a journal to record these verses and the ways He shows up in your life.

- **Be Still:** Create moments of quiet in your day to focus on His presence. Simply sit in stillness and allow yourself to feel His love.

- **Pray Honestly:** Share your burdens with God. Be honest about your struggles, doubts, and fears.

- **Practice Gratitude:** Make a habit of listing things you are grateful for daily. Gratitude shifts our perspective and helps us recognize His blessings.

- **Seek Community:** Surround yourself with others who encourage you in your faith journey. Hearing their testimonies of God's love can strengthen your own.

As you reflect on this chapter, take some time to consider these questions to help deepen your trust in God and your ability to rest in His love:

Reflection Questions:

1. What are some specific ways you've experienced God's love and faithfulness in your life?

2. What simple practices can help you create space to rest in God's love and release control?

3. In what areas of your life do you need to trust God more fully, and what steps can you take to surrender those to Him?

PART 3

Steps to Freedom: Learning to Live in His Perfect Love and Grace

"It is for freedom that Christ has set us free. Stand firm, then, and do not let yourselves be burdened again by a yoke of slavery."
Galatians 5:1

CHAPTER 9

You Are Not Alone

"So do not fear, for I am with you; do not be dismayed, for I am your God. I will strengthen you and help you; I will uphold you with my righteous right hand."
—Isaiah 41:10

Surrounded but Feeling Alone

Being in a crowd, like at church or in any social setting, can feel strange. You might be surrounded by people, but still feel completely alone. I have felt this more times than I'd like to admit. I often wonder how many other people feel this way without showing it. It's a silent struggle many might share, even if it's never openly expressed. We may think we are the only ones, but usually, we aren't.

Feeling alone is such a profoundly sad experience. The other day, I was driving and felt a bit alone in my journey. It was only for a moment, but those moments can be impactful. Feeling lonely has been part of my life for many years. It's not always about the absence of people, but about feeling unseen or unheard. You can sit in a crowded room or share a meal with loved ones and still feel like no one truly knows you. This kind of loneliness, the kind that comes from a lack of deep connection, is often harder to name and confront.

It's true that you can be surrounded by people who genuinely care about you and still feel utterly alone. How can this be? For me, it often comes from wrestling with questions that seem to have no answers. While I know God holds the answers and will guide me, lingering questions can leave an ache of loneliness in their wake because you don't feel safe and free to ask. This has been my experience. I am often afraid to ask questions because I don't know who to ask and, at the same time, know they won't judge me. Why am I afraid of judgment? Mostly because I don't want to be labeled as one of "those people" —the ones who kind of buck against traditions and form. I don't want to be rebellious or try to step out of God's line.

Loneliness arises when you think you are the only one who feels a certain way about things. It may be that you don't think anyone cares, and often people say they care, but do they really? In my community, I wonder how many people actually feel like they matter and that there is a place for them. Do they feel understood and cared for? It's important to seek understanding and offer it to others. Genuine connection can be a lifeline in the midst of isolation.

Wrestling with Questions

I've often grappled with questions about faith, church, and life–questions that have left me feeling isolated. In the religious tradition I grew up in, questioning was not encouraged. There was a pervasive sense that the answers had already been given, and questioning them was unnecessary, even wrong. Why challenge traditions that have been passed down for generations? Why question something that has been working for so long?

But I'd like to ask: if it's working so well, why do so many homes struggle to maintain harmony? Someone may say, "It's just how it is.

Humans make mistakes." That's true, but I feel like these struggles are too frequent and too deep to ignore.

Who is willing to step up and say, "You are not alone. These struggles, these questions, we have them too"? Who will be brave enough to say, "Me too"? I often feel that it's not that people don't care; rather, they don't know how to handle these hardships or what they are supposed to do about them. I've also wondered how much human interpretation has been interwoven with God's truth. What parts of religion reflect God's will, and what parts are merely cultural or traditional constructs? These questions can feel overwhelming. Who do you trust? Where do you go for clarity?

> *"Even though I walk through the darkest valley, I will*
> *fear no evil, for you are with me; your rod and your*
> *staff, they comfort me."* Psalm 23:4

Thankfully, there is one sure place: God and His Word. Scripture is the anchor that grounds us. Even then, I must be cautious. It's easy to read the Bible through the lens of how I was taught rather than with an open heart to God's true message. Ultimately, my desire is simple yet significant: to live a life that honors God, to love well, and to be like Jesus.

You Are Not Alone

While loneliness can feel overwhelming, it's important to remember the truth: you are not alone. In the past, I would have been afraid to share my deepest thoughts and questions, but I am learning that it is much better to open up. More often than not, I am not the only one with these thoughts or struggles.

So when you feel like hiding in a corner, convinced that you're the only one, remember—it's not true. This takes me back to the time when my new friend told me she wasn't afraid of my tears. I was sharing something very personal about my spouse and the struggles I was facing. It wasn't easy, but she had such a gentle demeanor that I felt safe opening up to her. I told her how I felt like I was second in his life, and of course, when that's what you believe, your brain starts looking for evidence to support it—you see what you expect to see.

Over time, I've come to realize that, yes, he had his struggles, but it wasn't my job to fix them. What he truly needed was my love, unconditional, without hidden expectations. And what I needed was to be okay with myself, love myself, and fully grasp that God loves me. He desires for me to have a happy marriage and a strong, healthy relationship with my spouse.

I've also learned that holding silent standards and expecting someone to automatically understand them is a recipe for disconnection. True connection comes through communication, grace, and the willingness to love without conditions.

Looking back on that conversation with my new friend, I now realize how powerful it was. Because of that moment, I have friends today who are my go-to people—the ones I trust to share with and be vulnerable. That experience taught me the power of being fully present and how vital it is to create safe spaces for others. It also reminded me that God often works through people to show His love and care.

> *"The Lord is near to the brokenhearted and saves the crushed in spirit."*   Psalm 34:18, ESV

Through moments like these, I have come to see that God is not only present in my quiet prayers but also in the warmth and kindness of the friends He places in my life. They are tangible reminders of His unwavering care. If you've ever felt alone, I encourage you to consider who God might have placed in your life to walk with you through those moments. Sometimes, the simplest act of reaching out can reveal the support you didn't realize was there. Scripture reminds us of God's constant presence:

> *"Be strong and courageous. Do not be afraid or terrified because of them, for the Lord your God goes with you; he will never leave you nor forsake you."*
> *Deuteronomy 31:6*

God's love surrounds us even when we can't feel it. That doesn't mean we're shielded from all harm or pain, but it does mean that we're never without His care and protection, even in ways we may never realize.

The Gift of Community

Loneliness often tempts us to isolate ourselves further, but God created us for connection. Practical ways to resist this temptation include intentionally reaching out to someone you trust, even if it feels difficult, or joining a small group or community activity where shared interests can foster relationships. Making a habit of praying for guidance and asking God to reveal opportunities for connection can also help. Additionally, being the one to offer a listening ear or a kind gesture can create bonds that not only ease your own loneliness but also bless others. As Ecclesiastes 4:9–10 says, "Two are better than one, because they have a good return for their labor: If either of them falls down, one can help the other up. But pity anyone who falls and has no one to help them up."

Recently, I heard a speaker talk about the importance of having "3 a.m. friends" that you can call in the middle of the night and know they'll be there for you. This idea resonated deeply, reminding me of God's presence as the ultimate "3 a.m. friend." No matter the hour, He is always near, ready to hear our cries and offer comfort. These earthly friendships are a reflection of His constant care.

Cultivating deep, meaningful friendships takes effort, but it's worth it. These relationships remind us that we're not alone. They're a tangible expression of God's love and care for us, a reflection of His unwavering, unconditional love. Even when these friends don't have all the answers to my questions or solutions to my struggles, their willingness to stand beside me is a testament to God's faithfulness. It's in these moments of shared presence that I am reminded of His promise to never leave or forsake us. True friendships, rooted in God's love, create a safe space where we can be ourselves, messy and imperfect, and still feel valued. These relationships don't just make life easier; they make life richer, as they offer a glimpse of the unending grace and care God extends to each of us.

Finding Purpose in Connection

Connection is the antidote to loneliness, a bridge that helps us move from isolation into a sense of belonging. It starts with recognizing the humanity in one another. My youngest sister once expressed her deep appreciation for how I could and would listen to her. She shared how much it meant to have someone truly hear her, and her gratitude has stayed with me as a reminder of the power of being present for others. Those moments have taught me that even the smallest gestures can create a ripple effect of hope and healing.

I find myself having deep, personal conversations with close friends, savoring every moment of connection. These exchanges leave me feeling refreshed, loved, and appreciated, a profoundly meaningful sensation that lingers long after our time together. Our purpose in connection is rooted in reflecting God's love to those around us.

Romans 12:15 reminds us: "Rejoice with those who rejoice; mourn with those who mourn."

This verse calls us to step into the lives of others, even when it's uncomfortable or inconvenient. It isn't easy getting involved with people whose lives get messy for reasons that they have no control over. Remember what you would like if these were the shoes you had to walk in.

I care deeply about supporting those who are struggling, especially in areas such as unhappy marriages and personal growth. These challenges can feel profoundly isolating, and I believe part of my purpose is to offer compassion, guidance, and hope. One reason I feel strongly about the importance of happy marriages is that I have seen firsthand the effects of unhappiness within a family. It leaves lasting shadows of regret and sadness that ripple through generations.

The ripple is challenging to stop, but it's another one of those things that has to be faced with courage, with someone willing to walk beside you. I have learned that offering support, even in small ways, can create a safe space for healing. Sometimes, it's simply being present, listening without judgment, or praying for those who feel trapped in their pain. These challenges can feel isolating, and I believe it's my purpose to offer support in whatever way I can.

Engaging with others in their struggles isn't easy or simple. It requires a willingness to stay committed for the long haul. But when we step into people's hardest moments with love and grace, we create opportunities for healing and transformation, not only for them, but for our communities as a whole. I long to see a more connected and supportive community, one where we bear one another's burdens as Christ calls us to do. Together, we can reflect His love and foster an environment of hope and renewal.

It's not always easy to connect deeply in a busy, fragmented world, but I believe God gives us the grace and opportunities to do so. Sometimes, it's as simple as asking someone how they really are and being willing to stay in that vulnerable space with them. This requires patience, humility, and a willingness to set aside our own agendas. True connection means listening not to respond, but to understand. Holding space is the practice of listening to someone with attentiveness and no judgment. It means holding space for someone's pain or joy without rushing to fix or dismiss it. I have friends who do this so well. I would encourage you to find some friends to hold space for you. It is a life-changing occurrence.

Holding space may not seem like a big deal to you, but when you are involved and you have that sacred space, you will value it so much. I remember a time when I reached out to a friend and I told her I was struggling. She listened to me without telling me what to do. When I was through talking, I felt so much better–not because I had all the answers, but because someone listened and seemed to understand me. She held space for me, and isn't that what God does for us? He knows our struggles, and He knows how hard it is, but He is waiting for us to come to Him, and He will comfort us.

We can be comforted through another person, which is a gift from God. There are times I can feel like God is far away, but when another human connects with me, it feels like a touch from Him. That connection could be as simple as a message saying, "Hey, I thought of you today," an invitation for coffee, or a walk together. These little touches matter so much in a world that often feels too busy for meaningful connections.

Moments like these remind me that even small acts of kindness and presence can have a profound impact. I've also had moments where I felt a nudge to call someone, and following through proved to be the right choice. The person I reached out to needed that connection, and it reinforced the importance of listening to and acting on those nudges from God. These small acts of obedience remind me that God uses us as instruments of His love and care. Even a simple phone call can create a lifeline for someone who feels unseen or alone.

They show us how God works through relationships to bring comfort and healing, reminding us that we are never truly alone. These moments, though small, have the potential to make someone feel seen, valued, and less alone. In doing so, we reflect God's love and remind ourselves that we, too, are part of a greater story of connection and grace.

Studies on the Toll of Loneliness

I know statistics tell us that loneliness is harmful to our overall health. Here are some things that came up when I checked on the studies of loneliness and health. Connection is key, and I believe connection is a God-designed gift for His children. These findings highlight how essential connection is for our well-being, reinforcing the truth that God designed us to thrive in relationships, with Him and with others.

Research has shown that loneliness is more than just an emotional experience—it has significant health consequences. Chronic loneliness is linked to elevated cortisol levels, which can contribute to hypertension, heart disease, and diabetes.[7] It also affects mental well-being, increasing the risk of depression, anxiety, and even cognitive decline. A 2019 study published in The Journal of Gerontology found that lonely individuals had a 40% higher risk of developing

---

7   Cacioppo, John T., et al. *Loneliness: Human Nature and the Need for Social Connection*. W.W. Norton & Company, 2015.

dementia.[8] Beyond mental and physical health, loneliness has been found to increase the risk of premature death by 26%.[9] Even in the workplace, loneliness negatively impacts job performance and satisfaction, as reported in Cigna's 2019 Loneliness Index.[10]

Loneliness Is Universal

Loneliness is a universal experience, but it doesn't have to define us. In God's presence and through meaningful connections, we can find hope and belonging. By leaning into our faith and investing in relationships, we reflect God's love to one another, creating a ripple effect of comfort and care.

Let us remember that even in seasons of feeling alone, we are part of a greater story of grace and community. In God's presence and through meaningful relationships, we can find hope, comfort, and belonging. While I may not have all the answers to my questions, I'm learning to trust God and cherish the connections He has placed in my life.

As I reflect on the power of connection, I am reminded of how Jesus modeled perfect love and belonging. He reached out to the lonely, the marginalized, and those who felt unseen. His example inspires us to step into the lives of others with courage and compassion, trusting that our small acts of love can make a significant difference. Whether it's a phone call, a shared meal, or simply listening without judgment, these moments are sacred and reflect God's heart for connections and building community.

---

8   Donovan, N. J., et al. "Loneliness and Risk of Alzheimer's Disease: A Prospective Study of the Health and Retirement Study." *The Journal of Gerontology: Series B*, vol. 74, no. 3, 2019, pp. 457-465.

9   Holt-Lunstad, Julianne, et al. "Loneliness and Social Isolation as Risk Factors for Mortality: A Meta-Analytic Review." *Perspectives on Psychological Science*, vol. 10, no. 2, 2015, pp. 227-237.

10 Cigna. *Cigna 2019 U.S. Loneliness Index.* Cigna, 2019, www.cigna.com/about-us/newsroom/2019/cigna-2019-loneliness-index.

What has always struck me about Jesus is how much He loved those who might have been hard to love. He looked past their surface demeanor and saw straight into their hearts. He loved them with a depth and tenderness that transformed lives. This stirs a longing in my heart to love others like Jesus did and to see beyond what is on the outside and truly care for the person within. I believe that as we strive to love this way, we reflect His presence in a world longing for connection and grace. Even in our smallest efforts, we can be vessels of His love, reminding others that they are never alone.

May we each strive to be the kind of friend who eases loneliness in others' lives, and may we rest in the assurance that we are never truly alone.

Reflection Questions:

1. When have you felt the most alone, and how did you experience God's presence during that time?
2. Who in your life might be feeling lonely, and how can you reach out to them in a meaningful way?
3. What steps can you take to cultivate deeper connections with both God and others?

CHAPTER 10

You Are Redeemed

---

*"In your unfailing love you will lead the people
you have redeemed."*
—Exodus 15:13

The Heart of the Gospel: Redemption

Redemption is the heart of the Gospel message. At its core, re-demption means to atone for, to rescue, or to set free. Spiritually, it signifies God's ultimate plan to restore us to Himself through the sacrifice of Jesus Christ. It's the bridge between our brokenness and God's perfection, made possible through Jesus Christ.

The Bible is rich with stories that illustrate the depth of re-demption, like the story of Naomi and Ruth. In this narrative, Boaz serves as their redeemer, a foreshadowing of how Jesus stands as our ultimate redeemer. Throughout Scripture, we see redemption in action: Joseph forgiving his brothers after their betrayal, Peter being restored after denying Jesus, and, most importantly, Jesus giv-ing His life to redeem humanity.

Redemption is not limited to a select few. It's God's invitation to all, extending His grace to the broken, weary, and lost, offering them a new beginning. It matters because it reminds us that no matter how far we've fallen, God's grace is always greater.

The journey to redemption begins with acknowledging our need for it. Redemption leads to a life of purpose, freedom, and peace. As we journey through this chapter, we'll uncover the profound truth of redemption and its power to transform our lives, relationships, and purpose. Let us explore this transformative truth more deeply.

Acknowledging the Need for Redemption

To embrace redemption, you first need to acknowledge your need for it. Sin creates a chasm between us and God, a separation we cannot mend on our own. This truth can be humbling, but it's a necessary step to open our hearts to God's grace. When we admit our shortcomings and surrender our pride, we make room for His redemptive work in our lives.

> *"For all have sinned and fall short of the glory of God."*
> *Romans 3:23*

Take a moment to reflect on your life. What areas feel distant from God? Write them down as a tangible act of confession, and trust that He will meet you there with mercy and love.

I remember feeling utterly unworthy, believing I could never measure up. While I tried to live without deep regrets, the weight of my imperfections seemed overwhelming. Despite knowing that we all fall short of God's glory, I didn't fully understand His willingness to redeem someone like me. It goes back to that flawed idea that I had to be perfect.

Over time, through prayer and help from other sources, I began to understand that we are all redeemable, and His love isn't dependent on my perfection but on His grace. Yet, laying my burdens before Him wasn't instantaneous; it was a gradual process. I understood these truths in my head, but they didn't connect with my heart right away. Redemption is not something we earn; it is a gift, unearned and undeserved, yet freely given.

My sister tried telling me that Jesus's sacrifice covers me, that through Him, we are free. Her words didn't resonate at first, but one day, while listening to someone read Romans 5:8, "But God demonstrates his own love for us in this: While we were still sinners, Christ died for us," this truth finally struck home. In that moment, I realized that I had been fighting a battle Jesus had already won, and the freedom that followed was life-changing. It can be the same for you. Life-changing moments are a big part of what Jesus can do for us.

It felt as though a door had been unlocked, and I was finally able to step into the light. I remember thinking, *How could I have missed this?* The weight I had been carrying was gone, and I felt as though I was a bird released from a cage, soaring for the first time. This is what being redeemed feels like. I didn't need to prove anything anymore; I was free to rest in His grace. It is a gift I cherish. I do have to be reminded of it every so often.

Perhaps you can relate to this struggle, or you may be just starting your journey. Wherever you are, trust that God's mercy will meet you, lifting your burdens and anchoring you in His unchanging love. As I continue to walk with Him, this truth becomes more real to me every day: His mercies are new every morning (Lamentations 3:22–23). No matter where you find yourself, God's mercy and grace are always waiting to restore and renew you.

The Gift of Grace Through Jesus

Through Jesus, God spans the chasm that separates us from Him, drawing us into His grace. Imagine Jesus standing between you and God, not as a barrier but as a shield, presenting you as spotless.

This truth became especially clear to me during a conversation with my daughter. As we were driving, she asked me about being good enough, and the thought came to me to share the scripture about Jesus's baptism. I told her how the dove rested on Him, and God said, "This is my Son, in whom I am well pleased." I explained to her that this is what Jesus is doing for her. God sees her through Jesus, and because of Him, God is well-pleased with her. She quietly accepted that explanation without hesitation, and it struck me how readily she trusted in that truth. It was a simple moment, but it reminded me of the beauty of God's grace and how He covers us completely through Jesus.

The song "Cover Me," composed by Mike Rogers and sung by Praise and Harmony, beautifully captures this vision of Jesus—covering you with His love, standing in your place—so that when God looks at you, He sees His beloved Son.[11] This is the essence of redemption. In those moments when the enemy tries to make you feel unworthy, remember: the battle has already been won. Accept the gift of atonement. You are redeemed. How wonderful it is to be made free!

> *"In him we have redemption through his blood, the forgiveness of sins, in accordance with the riches of God's grace."*   *Ephesians 1:7*

I picture redemption like the renewal of spring after the dormancy of winter. The air feels warmer, the once-barren trees begin to bud, and life stirs beneath the soil. When the world seems cold and lifeless, the first signs of spring bring hope, buds on the trees, flowers breaking through the soil, and the warmth of sunlight returning to the earth. Just as spring breathes new life into what

---

11 Rogers, Mike. "Cover Me." *Mighty God*, performed by Praise and Harmony, The Acappella Company, 2013.

seemed dead, God's redemptive power brings renewal and growth to our hearts. It's a transformation that turns barrenness into beauty, reminding us of His constant work in our lives.

> *"I have swept away your offenses like a cloud, your sins like the morning mist. Return to me, for I have redeemed you."*   Isaiah 44:22

Through Jesus, we are covered by grace and invited to step into the beauty of a redeemed life. Reflect on how His grace has brought renewal to your heart, much like the rebirth of spring. Let this truth sink into your heart: God's redemptive power is always at work, transforming what seems lifeless into something vibrant and full of purpose.

Living Redeemed: A Renewed Purpose

Redemption is not just an act; it's an invitation to rest in God's love, laying down the burdens of guilt, shame, and regret. God's love is vast and unconditional, inviting you to live unencumbered by the weight of the old you.

> *"Therefore, if anyone is in Christ, the new creation has come: The old has gone, the new is here!"*
> 2 Corinthians 5:17

When God redeems you, He doesn't just restore your heart—He equips you to bring hope and healing to others. Redemption transforms your relationships, enabling you to build connections rooted in grace and love. It empowers you to reflect God's glory in every interaction, creating ripples of peace and reconciliation that extend beyond yourself.

Redemption calls us to live as reflections of God's glory, shining His light into every area of our lives. Let go of the old and step into the new with confidence. You are redeemed, restored, and ready to fulfill His purpose for you.

> *"I have been crucified with Christ and I no longer live, but Christ lives in me. The life I now live in the body, I live by faith in the Son of God, who loved me and gave himself for me."* Galatians 2:20

This is God's promise: that through Jesus, you are empowered to live out your purpose with His light guiding every step.

Addressing Doubts and Embracing Grace

If you struggle to feel worthy of redemption, remember that it is not based on your merit but on God's mercy. I know how hard it can be to believe you're redeemable, especially when you feel stuck in old patterns or doubts. For too long, I wrestled with the idea that I had to be over certain struggles. But here's the truth: change takes time, and God's grace is sufficient for every step of the journey.

We all have default modes, habits, and mindsets that are hard to break. But with God, all things are possible. He meets us in our struggles, providing the grace and strength to move forward. It's a process, and while it's hard work, it's also a worthy work. As someone once told me, "Good, worthy work is always hard."

Finding resources to help us do this good work is another way to see faster progress. God often uses others to guide and encourage us, reminding us that we're not meant to carry our burdens alone. You also need friends working with you and supporting you on this path. It is so much better and almost easier to see growth if you don't do this alone. If you're not sure where to start, consider joining a small group at your church, reaching out to a trusted friend, or forming an accountability group.

Take the first step today: reach out to someone, share your journey, and invite them to walk alongside you. Together, you can grow in grace and strength, moving closer to the life God has called you to live.

I want to encourage you: don't let setbacks define you. God has already rescued you, bringing you out of darkness into light. Trust in His promises and lay your burdens down. Changes take time, and while we have our part to play, the ultimate work of redemption has already been completed by Jesus.

> *"For he has rescued us from the dominion of darkness*
> *and brought us into the kingdom of the Son he loves,*
> *in whom we have redemption, the forgiveness of sins."*
> *Colossians 1:13–14*

Embrace this truth: God's redemption is for everyone, including you. Walk boldly as a new creation, allowing the truth of your redemption to transform your life and inspire others to seek the same grace and peace.

Reflection Questions:

1. What doubts or old patterns are you holding onto that keep you from fully embracing God's redemption?
2. How can you remind yourself daily that God's work in you is ongoing and rooted in grace?
3. Who in your life might need to hear about the hope and renewal found in redemption, and how can you share it with them?

CHAPTER 11

Living Abundantly

> *"The thief comes only to steal and kill and destroy. I came that*
> *they may have life and have it abundantly."*
> *—John 10:10, ESV*

Seeking to Live an Abundant Life

The idea of an abundant life is beautiful. What comes to mind when you think of living abundantly? For me, it is love—so much love—peace, joy, and freedom. Freedom from stress and worry. Freedom to be who God created you to be. Freedom in living for Jesus, knowing He loves you immeasurably.

> *"Now to him who is able to do immeasurably more*
> *than all we ask or imagine, according to his power*
> *that is at work within us." Ephesians 3:20*

Abundance is not just about monetary success; it encompasses the intangible treasures of life. These are the things that matter most when our earthly journey ends: connections, deep friendships, thriving relationships, and memories created with loved ones. It's about instilling character traits that outlive us and leaving a legacy of love and faith.

Living abundantly also means letting go of the petty grievances and burdens we carry. Many of these things won't even matter in three to five years; yet, they have a way of keeping us locked up, often without our conscious awareness. True openness comes from feeling free, and true freedom comes through Jesus.

> *"The thief comes only to steal and kill and destroy; I have come that they may have life and have it to the full."*   John 10:10

If you contemplate the above verse and take it to heart, it makes you stop and acknowledge what a gift Jesus is offering us. He came so we may have life and have it to the full, or as some other translations say, "to have it abundantly." I love both versions. They are beautiful, hopeful, and speak to the possibility of a life that is meaningful and fulfilling.

Abundance is not about perfection or achieving everything we think we want. It's about appreciating the gifts God has already given us and trusting Him to lead us into the fullness of His promises. An abundant life invites us to live intentionally, embrace joy, and step into the freedom Jesus offers.

So, how can we live more abundantly? By focusing on what truly matters: faith, love, and the relationships that nurture our souls. By releasing the things that weigh us down and choosing to trust in God's provision and grace. Let us accept the gift of abundant life and live it with gratitude, purpose, and joy.

The Source of Freedom

Freedom is a gift—a gift Jesus freely offers us through His life, death, and resurrection. When you believe and accept His salvation, you will be free indeed.

"As far as the east is from the west, so far does he re-move our transgressions from us."
Psalm 103:12, ESV

Accepting this gift means embracing who you are in Christ and knowing that you are loved unconditionally. You are loved so deeply that your sins are no longer counted against you. What a profound and life-giving truth!

I've struggled with holding on to expectations, such high expectations I've had of people and situations. But what has this gained me? Certainly not abundance. I expected those in leadership, especially ministers and deacons, to be nearly flawless because they were so close to God. After all, they were called by Him to lead. I also carried certain expectations of my spouse, believing he was supposed to behave a certain way. But over time, I've come to see that God works in people according to His timing, not mine.

Interestingly, I don't hold everyone to those same high expectations. With some people, I freely give them space to mess up, yet with leaders and others in certain roles, I expect more. Maybe that's why the disappointments felt so deep—because I held them to a higher standard, believing they should always reflect God's wisdom and guidance. But they are human too. No one is perfect.

Letting go and releasing others from the weight of our expectations is a vital step toward living abundantly. It frees us to grow and pursue the relationships and environments that nurture us. As you evaluate your life, ask yourself: Are the people around me helping me grow, or are they holding me back? While we may not always have control over who is in our lives, we can set boundaries to protect our peace and well-being.

"It is for freedom that Christ has set us free. Stand firm, then, and do not let yourselves be burdened again by a yoke of slavery." Galatians 5:1

Your true source of freedom is Jesus. If you believe anything else, it's not true freedom. The devil will try to tell you that the only way to be free is to do things your way, but often that is what will lead you into bondage. Look to Jesus, the one who will give you what you are longing for: freedom and peace. It is true, and it is real.

Living with Boundaries

Boundaries are not walls; they are bridges to healthier, more authentic relationships. Saying "no" when necessary is an act of love, for yourself and for others.

> *"All you need to say is simply 'Yes' or 'No'; anything beyond this comes from the evil one."*
>
> *Matthew 5:37*

Honesty and clarity are kindness in action. Jesus Himself modeled this. He was direct and truthful, always speaking in love. We can follow His example by learning to say no with grace.

It's tempting to say yes to everything, especially when asked for help. But if your "yes" comes at the cost of your peace, your plans, or your growth, it might be time to reconsider. Saying no isn't selfish; it's wise stewardship of your time and energy.

Consider this: If you're constantly pouring into others but neglecting your own household or health, who truly benefits? Balance is essential. While good works are an integral part of the Christian life, they should not come at the expense of your own well-being or calling.

> *"Above all else, guard your heart, for everything you do flows from it."*
>
> *Proverbs 4:23*

When you first start to live with boundaries, it will not be easy, but keep at it, and soon it will become your new way of life. You may have to have some conversations to explain what is happening and why you are choosing to say no now when in the past you would have said yes. It may be difficult at first, and you may feel a little guilty, but remember Jesus had boundaries and He practiced them. Boundaries are so important for a healthy, abundant life.

Filling Your Cup

To live abundantly, you must take time to refill your spiritual and emotional cup. Spend time in God's presence, resting in His love.

> *"You prepare a table before me in the presence of my enemies. You anoint my head with oil; my cup over-flows."* Psalm 23:5

Take time to read His word, contemplate His promises, and reflect on how much He wants to be a part of your life. Engage in activities that bring you joy and renewal, whether it's taking a walk, diving into a sewing project, making food for family and friends, or baking bread (those are my go-to activities). Find yours and put your heart into it. The things that bring you joy are the gifts that God gave you to share with the world.

I used to feel like if I did anything for myself, it was wrong. I believed that only selfish people prioritize their own needs, and as a Christian, I thought I should always be focused on serving others. Somewhere along the way, I had picked up the idea that taking time for myself wasn't exactly a sin, but it felt dangerously close to one. It may sound extreme, but it was a serious belief in my mind—one of those unspoken rules I created and then lived by.

But over time, I've learned that when I take time to go out with friends, take a walk, or do something fun just for me, I can return to my family refreshed and more present. It is necessary to do things that fill our cup. These moments of joy and renewal help us to better nurture the life God has entrusted to us.

Filling your cup isn't selfish; it's about paying attention to what makes you feel alive and vibrant so you can pour into others from a place of fullness. Living abundantly isn't just about what you give; it's also about how you cultivate the joy and peace within yourself.

> *"But those who hope in the Lord will renew their strength. They will soar on wings like eagles; they will run and not grow weary, they will walk and not be faint."* Isaiah 40:31

Remember, what fills your cup will more than likely be what honors God. He made you, and He gave you those good desires and the ability to use them. Cultivating skills in areas where you may not be naturally gifted is also another way to fill your cup. Yes, sometimes there are things we don't enjoy doing, but it is life, and you have to do unpleasant things from time to time. A well-rounded life includes activities that bring you joy and some that just help you be a better person.

A Life Overflowing

Abundance is not an individual endeavor. It involves serving others and making a positive impact on their lives. However, it also requires recognizing your own needs and growth areas. Living abundantly means learning new skills, embracing change, and seeking tools that help you thrive. It's a constant process of learning, pivoting, and adjusting.

One of the most freeing truths is that Jesus' promise of abundance is not limited to this life. It extends into eternity. By living with purpose, loving others well, and serving God wholeheartedly, you create a life that overflows with meaning. You fulfill the abundant life Jesus came to give.

A life of abundance calls us to share our gifts and talents with the people of God and with everyone we meet. When we embrace abundance, we become kinder, more generous, and more empathetic. We are called to live a life overflowing with love and joy. The more I strive to have an abundant mindset, the more I experience peace and love in my life. It changes how I see people and the way I think about them.

I truly believe Jesus wants us to live with an abundant mindset. There is enough to go around—love, a place to belong, deep and lasting friendships, financial provision, and, most meaningful to me, grace.

Abundance isn't about how much we have; it's about how much we recognize God's hand in everything. It shifts our hearts from scarcity to gratitude, from fear to trust, and from holding back to pouring out. When we feel blessed, we become a blessing. We give our time more freely, we share our resources without hesitation, and we see others through the eyes of compassion.

A life of abundance is a life fully lived—one that overflows with love, faith, peace, generosity, and gratitude. This is what Jesus desires for us.

> *"And my God will meet all your needs according to the riches of his glory in Christ Jesus."*
> *Philippians 4:19*

I have learned that practicing gratitude helps me to see how much good I have in my life. Taking time for deep breaths and reflection also helps me to live well. Gratitude shifts my perspective, allowing me to focus on the blessings God has provided rather than the struggles I may face. Deep breaths and moments of reflection help me pause, realign my heart with God's truth, and approach life with renewed strength and peace.

It starts with recognizing the needs around us and stepping into the responsibilities God places before us. This doesn't mean living a life of constant busyness or saying yes to every request. Instead, it's about being intentional in our service, doing all things with joy, as if doing them for God. When we approach our tasks with this mindset, even struggles become opportunities for growth and deeper faith. And I would like to let you know it is my endeavor to live like this, but I don't always get it right.

Living abundantly means trusting that God's grace is sufficient for every challenge. It means viewing every act of service, every moment of struggle, and every small victory as part of a life well-lived. This perspective allows us to live within the "abundance range," a place where God's grace overflows into every aspect of our lives.

> *"In everything I did, I showed you that by this kind of hard work we must help the weak, remembering the words the Lord Jesus himself said: 'It is more blessed to give than to receive.'"*
>
> *Acts 20:35*

So, what kind of life will you choose to live? What steps will you take to create a life that overflows with meaning, joy, and purpose? Abundance doesn't happen by accident. It requires intentionality and faith. But as we align our hearts with God's, we begin to experience the fullness of His promise: a life overflowing with love, joy, and grace. It can be a beautiful and abundant life.

Stepping to Abundant Living

Living abundantly is not a distant dream or an unattainable goal; it is a promise from God and a gift that is already available to you. It begins with a heart anchored in His love, trusting that He has given you everything you need for a life of purpose, joy, and freedom.

> *"And God is able to bless you abundantly, so that in all things at all times, having all that you need, you will abound in every good work."*
> *2 Corinthians 9:8*

As you move forward, remember that abundance is found in the small, everyday moments: the laughter of loved ones, the beauty of God's creation, the quiet assurance of His presence. It is in choosing gratitude over grumbling, faith over fear, and love over judgment. These choices may seem simple, but they are profound acts of faith that open the door to a life overflowing with His grace. It takes courage to live and follow the truth.

Let your heart rest in the truth that God's abundance is limitless. He has given you not only the resources to live well, but also the strength to rise above challenges and the courage to embrace the life He has called you to live.

So take a deep breath, step forward in faith, and live boldly in the abundance of His love. Trust that He will meet you in every moment, filling your life with purpose, peace, and joy.

> *"Taste and see that the Lord is good; blessed is the one who takes refuge in him."*
> *Psalm 34:8*

May your life be a reflection of His abundant love, a light to others, and a testimony of His goodness. Abundance is not just what you receive; it is what you overflow. Go now and live in the fullness of His promise.

Reflection Questions:

1. What areas in your life feel abundant right now? Where do you need to trust God more?
2. How can you intentionally practice gratitude this week?
3. What gifts or talents has God given you that you can use to bless others?
4. But how do we do that? How do we embrace and live out this abundance?

CHAPTER 12

Be Who You Are Meant to Be

"As we let our own light shine, we unconsciously give other people permission to do the same."[12]
—Marianne Williamson

Who Are You Meant to Be?

God created you with a unique purpose. Your gifts, talents, and the way you see the world are unlike anyone else's. He designed you intentionally, not to be perfect or without fault, but to fulfill a role only you can fill. Mistakes and missteps are inevitable—we're born into a world full of people with tangled lives, shaped by the complexity of relationships and experiences.

Each family is a tapestry woven from the lives of its members, bringing together different histories, values, and ways of living. When two people marry and start a family, they carry into that home the threads of their upbringing. Often, these threads are vastly different. I know this to be true in my own marriage. How I was raised and how Terry was raised couldn't have been more different.

---

12 Williamson, Marianne. *A Return to Love: Reflections on the Principles of A Course in Miracles*. HarperOne, 1992.

But I've come to see that these differences don't have to divide us or hold us back from building strong marriages and relationships. Instead, they can teach us patience and grace. It's not always easy—I've struggled at times to navigate those differences. Yet, I've learned the value of giving space for the unique perspectives we each bring. This isn't just about compromise; it's about honoring the way God has shaped each of us.

When we embrace those differences and approach them with love and understanding, something beautiful happens. We create a home where diversity of thought and experience can coexist. Yes, it takes effort, and yes, it can be messy at times. But in that mess, we have the opportunity to reflect God's love by extending grace to one another.

So, as you consider who you are meant to be, remember that God's purpose for you is not tied to perfection. It's tied to love: love for Him, love for yourself, and love for the people He has placed in your life, even in their differences.

Woven by Grace: Embracing Your Unique Design

Have you ever paused to consider how intricately and purposefully God designed you? Every thread of your being reflects His artistry, and yet, life's challenges often make us doubt our significance. We face curveballs that leave us questioning our purpose, wondering who we are meant to be.

> *"For you created my inmost being; you knit me to-gether in my mother's womb."*   Psalm 139:13

I know those feelings well. There were seasons in my life when I wrestled with doubts about my impact, my worth, and whether

I truly had a place in God's grand design. The weight of those questions was heavy, and the answers didn't come overnight. But through years of seeking, praying, and personal growth, I've come to a comforting realization: God made me for a reason.

His hands wove me together with intention, and He has a plan for me—a plan that isn't thwarted by life's detours or my imperfections. I can rest in that truth. I don't have to strive or struggle to figure it all out on my own. Instead, I can trust that as I follow Him, I am becoming exactly who He meant me to be.

The same is true for you. Whatever doubts or uncertainties you carry, know this: you are a masterpiece in progress, designed by the Creator Himself. You don't have to have all the answers today. Rest in the fact that God has a plan for you, and He is faithful to complete the work He's started in you. Let go of the doubt. Lean into His grace. And trust that you are exactly where you are meant to be, woven by grace and held in His love.

From Tangles to Triumph: Trusting God's Hand

Life often feels like a tangled web of threads—messy, confusing, and far from beautiful. For much of my journey, I couldn't imagine anything good coming from my life story. Let alone beautiful, from the failures and missteps that seemed to define my path. But over time, God has shown me His incredible power to redeem even the most tangled threads. He knew where each thread needed to go and how to weave them into what He could see was going to be a testament of His faithful love.

> *"And we know that in all things God works for the good of those who love him, who have been called according to his purpose."* Romans 8:28

What once seemed like a hopeless mess has become a tapestry of His grace, woven together for a purpose beyond anything I could have imagined. He takes our failures, our pain, and even our doubts, and creates something useful and beautiful. Far too many years were spent balking at how I was and what seemed like drawbacks, but now I see them as my superpower. I used to hate my smile because I thought it was too big. My aunt would comment on it every time she saw it, and her words made me self-conscious. But now, people tell me my smile is one of my best features, a bright spot that draws them in.

I also used to feel ashamed of being so sensitive, as if it were a flaw. But over time, God has shown me that my sensitivity is a gift. It allows me to be more attuned to others, to notice their feelings and needs, and to respond with compassion. What I once saw as a weakness, I now recognize as a strength that helps me connect with others on a deeper level.

God has been teaching me to see myself through His lens—one of love, purpose, and intentional design. He has reminded me that every detail, from my big smile to my sensitive heart, is part of how He created me to reflect His love and care. What a gift it is to know that even the things I once tried to hide can be used for His glory.

This process of transformation isn't quick or easy. I've learned that it's a lifelong journey, one of surrender, trust, and continual growth. And while I'm still a work in progress, I've come to see that being a work in progress is something to be proud of. It's a testament to God's ongoing work in my life, His faithfulness in shaping me into who I'm meant to be.

As you reflect on your own journey, take a moment to acknowledge where you've been. Celebrate the progress you've made, the triumphs you've achieved, and even the failures that have taught you valuable lessons. Every thread, no matter how tangled, has a purpose in His hands.

Remember, the masterpiece God is creating in you isn't finished yet. Trust His hand, and know that He is working all things for good, weaving a story of redemption and beauty that only He can create.

The Master Weaver: Finding Strength in Your Story

I used to wish for an easy, flawless life—a home where everything went smoothly and challenges were few. But as I've walked through life's ups and downs, I've come to see that the struggles we endure are what shape us. They make us stronger, wiser, and more compassionate. Life is undeniably hard, but it's also a beautiful journey of growing and becoming.

> *"He has made everything beautiful in its time."*
> *Ecclesiastes 3:11*

I've learned to embrace the hard parts of my story, not as curses, but as gifts. These trials have been tools in God's hands, helping me grow into the person He designed me to be. If I hadn't faced those struggles, who would I be today? It's a question I ask myself, not because I need an answer, but because it reminds me to value every part of my journey, the joys and the hardships alike.

Your story, too, is a gift. Even the painful chapters carry treasures. They bring resilience, perseverance, endurance, strength, and courage. And oh, how much courage it takes to step into uncertainty, to face the unknown, and to allow God to lead you into the person He is calling you to become!

So, love your story—all of it. Embrace the gifts it has brought into your life. Trust that God, the Master Weaver, is creating something beautiful and meaningful, even in the hardest moments. Your story isn't finished yet, and in His time, He will make all things beautiful.

Threads of Purpose: Living Authentically in Him

We are all uniquely designed by God, created with purpose and intention to fulfill a specific role in His plan. You have a place in this world—a space only you can fill. You don't need endless tests or assessments to uncover who you are, though tools like these can sometimes help us better understand ourselves. What's most important is recognizing that your ideas, your perspective, and the way you approach life are gifts from God.

> *"For we are God's handiwork, created in Christ Jesus to do good works, which God prepared in advance for us to do."*   *Ephesians 2:10*

Your uniqueness is something to be celebrated. It's a reflection of God's creativity and His deep care in designing you exactly as you are. No one else sees the world just as you do, and that's no accident. God made you with intention, and He delights in seeing you shine in the gifts and talents He has given you.

You are the created, and He is the Master Designer. He has prepared good works for you, and He invites you to step boldly into your purpose. Lean into the identity He's given you and live it out with confidence, knowing that He is with you every step of the way. When you trust in His design and walk in His purpose, your life becomes a reflection of His glory—a beautiful tapestry of faith, love, and impact.

Unraveled Yet Redeemed: Freedom in Being Known

The truth of redemption is one that bears repeating—it's a beautiful, life-changing gift from Jesus, and we must never take it for granted. Through His sacrifice, we are redeemed, set free, and deeply loved.

> *"Now the Lord is the Spirit, and where the Spirit of the Lord is, there is freedom."*
>
> *2 Corinthians 3:17*

When life feels like it's unraveling, when the threads of your world seem to be coming apart, remember whose you are. You are a child of God, redeemed by His grace. Even in the moments when it feels like everything is falling apart, His love holds you together.

Your unraveling isn't the end of the story. In God's hands, it becomes the beginning of something new and beautiful. He makes a way where there seems to be none, and He invites you to step into the freedom that comes from being fully known and fully loved by Him.

No matter how unraveled your life may seem, you are never beyond His reach. Redemption is His promise, and freedom in Him is your birthright. What a beautiful, wonderful gift to know that you are His, redeemed and free. Rest in that truth, and let it shape your heart and your life.

The Fabric of Faith: Strength in Community

Community is one of the most beautiful gifts we receive as God's children. But "community" doesn't have to mean hundreds of people. In my experience, just two or three close friends, friends who truly love and support you, can make all the difference when your world feels like it's falling apart.

> "Though one may be overpowered, two can defend themselves. A cord of three strands is not quickly broken." Ecclesiastes 4:12

There's incredible strength in having even a small group of people who remind you of God's faithfulness, who walk with you through life's challenges, and who celebrate your victories. These friendships are precious threads in the fabric of your faith, helping you see God's hand even in the hardest moments.

Find your people. Build your tribe, no matter how small, with God at the center. Together, you'll create a bond that is strong, unshakable, and rooted in His love. In those few trusted relationships, you'll find the strength to face life's trials and the joy of sharing its blessings.

Unfinished Yet Beloved: Trusting the Process

I've often talked about embracing, loving, and trusting the process because we are all unfinished works in progress. It's not always fun to be in the middle of struggles or to realize that you've messed up—again. But I've learned to look at these moments differently, to see them as gifts. They are opportunities to learn, to grow, and to experience God's grace in action.

God is completing a good work in you. Even when it feels messy or overwhelming, He is shaping you into the person He created you to be. The struggles, the setbacks, and the victories are all part of His perfect plan. Though we may not always see it, He is weaving together something beautiful, and He will bring it to completion in His perfect time.

So, when the process feels hard, remember to pause and reflect. Embrace the lessons, love the growth, and trust that God's hand is guiding you every step of the way. You are unfinished, yes, but you are also beloved. Rest in the confidence that the One who started a good work in you will be faithful to complete it.

Living the Design: Courage to Be You

Living authentically as the person God designed requires courage. It means trusting in His love and purpose for your life, even when the journey has been challenging. Every hardship you've endured, every triumph, and every struggle have played a role in shaping who you are today.

> *"For the Spirit God gave us does not make us timid, but gives us power, love and self-discipline."*
> *2 Timothy 1:7*

Having the courage to embrace both your strengths and your weaknesses is a gift. It's not about pretending to be perfect; it's about recognizing how God can use every part of your story for His glory. When you see your strengths, you can step into them confidently. When you acknowledge your weaknesses, you allow God to work through them, shaping you into someone even stronger in faith and character.

God has a way of weaving purpose through even the craziest and most difficult parts of life. He takes the threads of your experiences, both the good, the hard, and uses them to create something beautiful. Living out your design means embracing all of it with courage and stepping boldly into the life He's called you to live. This could mean serving others with your gifts and talents that bring you joy and fulfillment, setting boundaries that allow you to live with peace and purpose rather than people-pleasing, embracing the unique passions and interest God placed in you and trusting it is all part of His plan, and releasing fear of failure and stepping boldly into the dreams He has given you.

When you live in your design, you reflect God's glory and inspire others to do the same. You become a beacon of His love, power, and grace, a living testament to His faithfulness.

A Tapestry of Hope: Thanking the Past, Embracing the Future

Your past is a part of your story, a tapestry woven with moments of joy, struggle, growth, and learning. It's natural to look back and wish you had done things differently, to see missed opportunities or mistakes. But remember this: you did the best you could with what you knew at the time.

> *"Forget the former things; do not dwell on the past.*
> *See, I am doing a new thing!"*   Isaiah 43:18–19

Instead of dwelling on what could have been, choose to look at your past with gratitude. Thank God for the lessons learned, the strength gained, and the grace that carried you through. Every moment, even the difficult ones, has been used by Him to shape you into who you are today.

Acknowledging the past with gratitude doesn't mean denying pain or pretending it didn't happen. It means recognizing that God's hand has been at work, redeeming and transforming even the hardest parts of your journey. It's a beautiful step toward freedom, allowing you to step into the future without the weight of regret or shame.

God's promise is one of renewal and hope. The future awaits you, full of possibilities and guided by His loving presence. As you move forward, lean into His promise that He will never leave you or let you down. He stands right beside you, offering His strength, wisdom, and endless love.

The past has its place, but it doesn't define you. With God as your ultimate source and guide, your future holds infinite hope and promise. He's doing a new thing—can you see it? Trust Him, take His hand, and step boldly into the life He has for you.

Yes, there will always be things you could have done better, but God doesn't ask for perfection; He asks for your heart. Now that you know better, you can do better, and He will equip you with everything you need for the journey ahead. It is a true gift. I like action steps, so here are a few for you to consider:

- **Release the Past:**
    - Spend time in prayer, asking God to help you let go of any lingering guilt, regret, or bitterness. Trust that He has already forgiven you and is calling you to something new.

- **Reflect with Gratitude:**
    - Write down moments from your past that have taught you something valuable or revealed God's faithfulness. Gratitude helps shift your perspective and prepares your heart for what lies ahead.

- **Step into the New:**
    - What is the "new thing" God is calling you to? Is there a dream, a relationship, or a purpose He's placing on your heart? Take small, faithful steps toward it, knowing He walks with you every step of the way.

Releasing the past is such a huge step into freedom, then reflect with gratitude, another strong marker of making your life so much better, and last but not least, step into the "new" whatever God is asking of you, trust, and follow through.

Reflection Questions:

1. What are the gifts and abilities God has uniquely placed in you?

2. How can you use your experiences, even the hard ones, to encourage or support others?

3. Are there areas where fear or self-doubt might be holding you back from stepping into your God-given design?

Conclusions

*"I now see how owning our story and loving ourselves through
that process is the bravest thing that we will ever do."*[13]
—Brené Brown

A Journey Towards Grace and Learning to Embrace God's Unconditional Love

As we conclude this journey together, I invite you to pause and reflect on the threads of God's love that weave through your life. This book has been about exploring questions, struggles, and joys, all within the context of His unwavering presence. It is a testament to the grace that sustains us and the unconditional love that meets us wherever we are.

Throughout the pages, we've seen how loneliness, doubt, and confusion can challenge our faith and sense of belonging. Yet, in the midst of these trials, God's love shines through. It is there in the quiet moments of prayer, in the kindness of a friend, and in the truths of His Word.

As Psalm 139:7–10 reminds us, "Where can I go from your Spirit? Where can I flee from your presence? If I go up to the heavens, you are there; if I make my bed in the depths, you are there. If I rise on the wings of the dawn, if I settle on the far side of the sea,

---

13 Brown, Brené. *The Gifts of Imperfection: Let Go of Who You Think You're Supposed to Be and Embrace Who You Are.* Hazelden Publishing, 2010.

even there your hand will guide me, your right hand will hold me fast."

God's love is not something we earn or deserve; it is a gift freely given. This message has often been repeated in this book, but it is an important message to remember. In a world that often measures worth by accomplishments and perfection, God invites us to rest in the assurance that His love is constant and unchanging. This truth is a lifeline, reminding us that no matter how far we wander, we are never beyond His reach.

Embracing God's Love in Our Journey

Living in the reality of God's love transforms how we see ourselves and others. It frees us from the weight of expectations and empowers us to extend grace. It's not about having all the answers or living a flawless life, but about walking humbly with God, trusting Him to guide our steps.

Consider the challenges you've faced, the doubts you've wrestled with, and the questions that remain unanswered. Can you see glimpses of God's love woven into those moments? Perhaps it was a timely word from a friend, a sense of peace in prayer, or the realization that you were never truly alone.

As Romans 8:38–39 beautifully states, "For I am convinced that neither death nor life, neither angels nor demons, neither the present nor the future, nor any powers, neither height nor depth, nor anything else in all creation, will be able to separate us from the love of God that is in Christ Jesus our Lord."

Moving Forward

As you close this book, I encourage you to carry its lessons into your daily life. Let the assurance of God's unconditional love be the foundation upon which you build. Seek His presence in the ordinary moments, and let it shape how you love and serve others. Remember:

- **God's love is constant.** No circumstance can diminish it.

- **Grace is sufficient.** It meets you in your weakness and empowers you to grow.

- **Connection matters.** Reflect God's love through kindness and compassion to those around you.

Final Reflections

This journey is not about arriving at perfection, but about walking faithfully with the One who loves you unconditionally. Let this be a reminder that God's love is woven through every chapter of your life, the joys, the sorrows, and the questions. You are seen, known, and deeply loved.

As you step into the next chapter of your life, may you do so with courage and grace, secure in the knowledge that you are never alone. And may the love of God guide you, sustain you, and inspire you to live fully and love deeply.

With gratitude and hope,
Erna Boehs